Development and Sustenance of
Reading Habit

Development and Sustenance of

Reading Habit

Woven Around
the Nucleus of Ideas of
Prof. K.S. Deshpande

by
Dr S. K. Savanur

Reference Press
Delhi

First Edition 2010

Published by SUMIT SETHI
for **Reference Press**
4837/24, Ansari Road, Darya Ganj,
New Delhi - 110 002
Ph. : 23260807, 41563444
Fax : 011-41563334
E-mail: info@essessreference.com
url:http://www.essessreference.com

ISBN : 978-81-7000-632-9

Price : 425/-

Laser Typesetting:
Mukesh Graphics
T-1264, Mangolpuri, New Delhi
Ph. : 011-27918550, 9899079035
E-mail:mukeshgraphics29@yahoo.com

Printed at :
Print Line

This work is dedicated

To

Prof. B.B. Hungund

who had once told me,

"It is better to be a day early, than a minute late."

Contents

Preface

This book is a reflection of Prof. K.S. Deshpande's concern for quality library services and development of reading habit among youngsters.

Prof Deshpande is a mentor for many of us. His inspiring lectures punctuated with brilliant quotations and embellished with anecdotes from the lives of great men and women are still reverberating in my ears. I am sure, thousands of his students and readers of the five University Libraries which he developed in Karnataka will whole heartedly agree with my observations.

The concept of this book is developed around the nucleus of these quotations, anecdotes and stray ideas expressed by him in different occasions. I have interpolated certain ideas based on my experience (1974 to 1989) at the British Council Library, Chennai, at the Western Regional Instrumentation Centre, Mumbai and at the Department of Library and Information Science (LIS), Joshi-Bedekar College, Thane.

The book is about developing and sustaining reading habit. To achieve this mission certain things have to be done at individual level and others, at the institutional and government level.

The first part of the book constitute more than 80% of the content, and it is addressed to parents, teachers, librarians and students who work at individual level to promote reading habit of their own and/or that of others. This is 'bottom-up' approach for developing reading habit at the individual level.

The next part of the book is about book-trade, education, literacy, library system etc., which take care of 'Top-down' approach to reading habit. This is the effort to be done at institutional level. The book includes a chapter on reading habit in relation to Information and Communication Technology (ICT), forming the third part.

This is not a scholarly book on reading habit, hence, there are not too many references. It is based on my experience and observation supported by my reading on this subject. The thoughts are rational and mission-oriented Therefore, the approach is straight to the point and practical.

I thank Prof K.S Deshpande for being a great mentor. He made all of us proud of being librarians. Many of us owe our careers to him.

This book is a joint effort of Prof K.S.Deshpande Endowment Lecture Committee. Prof. Hungund and Dr S.R.Ijari's silent support was at the back of this work. Mr G.B.Hombal chased me whenever I was a little slow during this project.

Dr K.N. Prasad, the Convener of the Committee, has not only encouraged me to proceed with this work, but also read all the chapters and given invaluable suggestions. Without his value addition this book would not have been what it is now. I thank him for the faith he has in me.

I thank Prof. J.V. Naik for his foreword. It has added great value to this project.

The entire Committee is thankful to Mr Sumit Sethi, Chief Executive, Ess Ess Publications, for making the copies available at the right time.

Developing reading habit, training people in searching web-based information etc. are the missions for most of us working for Prof. K.S.Deshpande Endowment Lecture Committee. This work is one step in that direction, and the mission continues.

Happy reading.

Dr. S.K.Savanur
Dept. of LIS
Joshi-Bedekar College, Thane
Contact: sksavanur@rediffmail.com
M. : 098201 50352

Foreword

Education is the key to advancement in life. The pioneers of the Nineteenth century Indian Renaissance beginning with Raja Rammohun Roy, had realized that for the achievement of national emancipation, it was necessary to take education to the grass-root level throughout the length and breadth of this ancient land of ours. In the pursuit of this objective the founding fathers of Indian National Movement aimed at universal education by making elementary education free and compulsory throughout the country. This very ideal is enshrined in the Directive Principles of State Policy enunciated in the Indian Constitution.

Education is an ongoing and unending process, and it can be sustained only by cultivating reading habit among people belonging to all sections and strata of our society. And, it was for this purpose that in 1972, the Silver Jubilee Year of Indian Independence, and the "International Book Year", which also happened to be the bi-centenary year of the birth of Raja Rammohun Roy, the Government of India established Raja Rammohun Roy Library Foundation (RRRLF) to support public library services and system and library movement throughout the country. The declared objective of this movement was to promote reading habit among the masses for betterment of their life. The Foundation is a living memorial to the great Raja who heralded the modern age in India.

Dr S. K. Savanur deserves to be complimented and congratulated on his bringing out this extremely useful and valuable book dealing with almost every aspect, including technology, of developing and sustaining reading habit. In this relatively slim volume, he covers in a concise, clear and creative manner everything concerning reading - what, when and how to read and also the purpose and method of reading at several different stages of human development, from the childhood to the evening of one's life. Written in a lucid language and simple style, the book makes an easy and pleasant reading. It is as interesting as it is instructive.

For this commendable intellectual exercise, Dr Savanur does not claim for himself any originality of thought or approach. He humbly states that the entire book is "Woven around the Nucleus of Ideas of Prof. K. S. Deshpande", a living legend in the field of Library Science and Services, at whose feet he was privileged to learn the basics of Librarianship and of Book Culture, and also the crucial role that the librarian is expected to play in dissemination of knowledge and, by the same token, in nation-building.

This book of great practical value should be placed not merely at the hands of every teacher, librarian and student but also that of the lay-reader with a view to serving a wider purpose envisaged by the architects of the Indian Constitution, and the crusaders of social justice.

I have no doubt that the demand for the book of this sort would be so great that a second edition will be soon called for.

Mumbai
July 10, 2010

J.V. Naik
Professor & Head (Retd)
Department of History,
University of Mumbai
Member, Advisory Committee
National Book Trust, India
Former Member of the Raja Rammohun
Roy Library Foundation

1

READING HABIT : AN INTRODUCTION

Stephen Covey, a Harvard educated Management Guru has identified and propagated *Seven Habits of Highly Effective People* in his bestseller of the same title. It is estimated that over 15 million copies are sold all over the world. These seemingly simple habits are as follows.

1. Be proactive
2. Begin with the end in mind
3. Put first things first
4. Think win-win
5. Seek first to understand and then to be understood
6. Synergize
7. Sharpen the saw

Each habit has great philosophy behind it. There is large output of published literature about each habit. Many commentaries are written about Stephen Covey's book. Millions of web pages, PowerPoint presentations, tutorials and pdf files are written about these habits. Nevertheless, the first time anyone comes across these habits, he/she can easily sense what is connoted by the first six laws. But the seventh habit is a little difficult to comprehend.

The seventh habit deals with keeping our tools in a ready-to-use condition. The 'tool' here is both physical and figurative. It deals with self-renewal and updating ones own knowledge and understanding. It could be by reading, listening, discussing, observing or viewing television, surfing the net, experimenting, among many other similar processes of acquiring knowledge.

We live in the information age; we live in a knowledge society. Shopping, banking, teaching, learning and many other social transactions are done through information exchange. It is essential for everyone to read more and more for survival. Well, the focus of this work is on reading, rather on the habit of reading.

Habit is that which we enjoy doing. It is that activity which is done effortlessly. Habits are routine, repetitive behaviours. Habits are not instinctive like hunger or thirst. These are learned.

Reading is a habit. Like any other, it is an acquired habit. But, how does one acquire reading habit and sustain it? Well, it is a Pandora's box. It may open a can of worms. To be literate is one thing and to read is another. Reading is a complex socio-psychological process.

But surely there are simpler and inexpensive solutions for this complex question of developing and sustaining reading habits. This book attempts to give simple, affordable and practicable ideas.

At the outset, it is necessary to remind ourselves the proverb, '**You can lead a horse to water, but you can't make him/it drink.**' This means you can give someone the opportunity to do something, but you cannot force the person to do it if he/she does not want to do it. The proverb describes the problem of developing and sustaining reading habit.

At one end it is necessary to provide the necessary infrastructure like good library system, encouraging book trade, school and education system, parental support etc. This is leading a horse to water. Although there are many hurdles, this can be carried out somehow. But making the horse drink water is much more complex. Developing reading habit involves motivating potential readers, looking into various other things which go by the mood of the reader to be.

This book is divided into three parts.

The first part deals with making the horse drink. Therefore, motivational aspects are taken first. This is something that has to be done at an individual's level. Children, youth, parents, teachers, librarians etc have a role in it. This does not need any Government support. This is to be carried out at micro level. More emphasis is laid on this aspect.

The second part is more about leading the horse to water. It talks of the Government and institutions' role. The aspects of developing and sustaining reading habit are scattered in both the parts. However, the first part is primarily dealing with developing the reading habits and the second is more about sustaining them.

The third part deals with reading habit in the context of Internet and television era. This has more to do with Information and Communication Technology

Thus, the text will be evolved in the following chapter scheme.

A. **Developing Reading Habits**
   - What motivates people to read?
   - Children and Reading
   - What to read and When to Read
   - Reading purposes: For information, amusement,

recreation, knowledge, wisdom, teaching, writing etc.

- Reading Techniques: Reading newspapers (news items, editorials, features, advertisements book reviews, film reviews, etc.), textbooks, poetry, reference books, reading loudly, for exhaustive study, Reading Speed
- Reading and Comprehension

B Sustaining Reading Habit

- Book Trade, Nature/Types of books [Picture Books, 3-D Books, Talking Books, Comics, Abridged editions of Classics etc.] Bookshops. Education, Literacy, Encouragement from Parents, Teachers. Methods such as School Projects, Visits to Libraries, Bookshops and Book Exhibitions etc.
- Public Libraries; Government's Role, School/College Libraries

C. Reading Habit in Internet Era

Internet and TV are not enemies of reading. These are different means of acquiring information/knowledge. All these coexist and supplement each other. Parents and teachers should watch TV programmes or surf the net with children. This helps in developing better reading taste among children.

The following chapters look into these topics dealing with why, when and how aspects of developing reading habits.

Part A :

Developing Reading Habit

2

What Motivates People to Read?

Reading does not come natural to a human being. It has to be acquired. It needs to be cultivated. One needs to practice and develop the skill. We must understand what happens when a child learns to read at the early stages.

Initially a child associates an object for an alphabet, such as A for Apple, B for Bat etc. Then, it associates a text for an object. At this stage, it is the word or the text 'CAT' which is associated with the animal 'cat'.

A child's world is full of things that can be sensed with the five sensory organs. Thus, the word 'mango' is associated with a shape, colour, smell taste etc. The word 'parrot' is associated with an animal that can fly, that is of green colour, that has a red, hook-like beak with ability to imitate human speech.

At this stage, i.e. six to ten or twelve years of age, the texts for children are accompanied by pictures. Initial books like comics hold attention, as there is less of text and more of visuals in them. So long as such association is happening, a child enjoys reading and listening to stories. Books written and designed for this age group help in exploring the world around in small doses. Such books develop a child's thinking and imagination.

Some problems with reading begin as the child grows.

2.1. HURDLES FOR READING

As a child steps into teen years, a few things happen, which affect the reading process. Reading, which used to be a pleasure pastime, gradually becomes a burden. Some of the reasons for this transformation can be listed as follows.

- Illustrations / visuals start giving way to more of text in the books meant for growing kids.
- The content that a child is asked to read includes more and more abstract ideas such as 'right', 'wrong', 'love', 'justice' etc which do not hold the kid's attention. These things need child's effort to comprehend.
- A child is expected to concentrate more on formal education related material which requires reading of uninteresting mundane information for examinations.
- A child, which was hitherto reading loudly, pronouncing each word properly, is asked to read silently as it grows. This is a mental activity requiring more concentration which is difficult for a child.
- The amount of reading to be done increases, visual content reduce in number and font size becomes smaller. All these make reading a boring exercise.
- A child at this stage is naturally attracted towards sports, games, friends, movies, music etc.
- Many other distractions such as smoking, gambling, easy money-making and other vices and truths of life appear more important to a child. This is compounded by lack of attention from parents; they are busy building their own career.

These are seven major reasons for loss of interest in reading. [Of course, there are many other social reasons like child labour, child marriage, etc which contribute to the loss of interest in general reading.] If a child can overcome and/ or is helped by someone to cross these hurdles, reading habit can be cultivated or developed.

If these mind-blocks are not removed, the child fails to develop liking for reading as it grows. As an adult, he/she loses interest in reading due to other pressing priorities such as family responsibilities, professional pressures etc. Although reading materials are around, he/she may not show interest in them. Even if he picks up a book, he/she may not sustain interest in reading.

Therefore, it is necessary to motivate both children and adults to read.

2.2. WHO SHOULD MOTIVATE TO READ AND WHY?

It could be anybody. It could be parents, teachers, librarians, friends, spouses and above all, lives of great people.

Parents, teachers, librarians, bosses may inspire or motivate to read directly. They have genuine interest in the potential readers. But, why should someone motivate others to develop reading habits?

Parents feel that their child should be equipped with knowledge to face the world. Some parents consider their children as their investment. There is a misplaced notion that more education leads to more money. Parents no doubt motivate, but they may insist more on scholastic reading. Some parents who are interested in all-round growth of their children balance both general and scholastic learning.

Teachers' duty is to develop independent learning skills in children. Teachers' success is measured by students' performance. Therefore, they motivate students to read. Teachers insist on both scholastic and general reading.

Librarians provide a variety of reading material to children and adults. They have a long-term interest in developing reading habit. In marketing parlance, readers are the customers of libraries. Librarians feel happy when their books are put to maximum use. Librarians introduce students to situational reading. [See p. 55-56 for Reading Purposes]

Friends (spouse included) motivate to read, as they are interested in our development. They are our well-wishers. They want to share certain ideas in its original form.

While all these people have some direct interest in developing reading habit, great men and their works inspire without any other interest. They have made their contributions to the society. It is we who seek to get motivated.

All the above stated motivations come from outside. But, there are many who are self-motivated. They are curious to understand the world around them. And even the external motivation also ultimately leads to self-motivation.

2.3. HOW TO MOTIVATE?

Motivation for reading can be extrinsic or intrinsic. Different people require different types of triggers. Different strokes for different folks, as it is said. Broadly speaking, there are two types of motivations for reading.

- Extrinsic Motivation
- Intrinsic Motivation

It is necessary to examine these two motivations.

a. Extrinsic Motivation

Extrinsic motivations are those acts which are not inherent. It is in the form of rewards for reading. Rewards could be in the form of a gift or pampering or a social control factor.

Such external or extrinsic motivations are ideal in childhood or even in adolescence. A chocolate or an ice-cream or a movie could be a good motivator in these formative years.

Participation in an elocution, debate competition and scholastic projects etc. also provide extrinsic motivation for reading.

As the child gets into adolescence, even the nature of gift for birthday or getting a first division or any other achievement etc, (not for reading) should change. It could be one-year membership for a public library or gift coupons of a bookshop etc.

While a child can be motivated with the above options, an adult needs different types of motivation.

External motivations for grown ups could be a forthcoming competitive examination or an interview. He may read because a few books are prescribed, and he does not want to fail. Compliance, recognition, promotion in employment, competition and a deliberate attempt to impress someone are extrinsic motivations. There is another less known, but prominent extrinsic factor that prompts reading; it is a tendency to avoid work or a complex challenge. In other words, avoid work or challenges in the pretext of reading.

There is a word of caution. Take care that the child does not get addicted to gifts. Throughout life one can not go on giving gifts. Gradual move from gifts to appreciation to social identity is necessary for developing reading habit. Ultimately, a child and adult should know that reading is a reward in itself. He/she should know that reading gives a sense of accomplishment. This leads us to intrinsic motivations.

b. Intrinsic Motivations

With incentives one can trigger reading interest. But, it can not be sustained. Incentives have a limit. Continued interest in reading will come from intrinsic wants and needs. Enhanced reading competency and accomplishment are rewards in themselves.

We should read because we want to read; we need to read and not because we are asked to read. But, why do we want to read? (*http://www.readingrockets.org/research/topic/motivation*).

The answer is self-efficacy. Self-efficacy is the ability of a person to judge his own capabilities with regard to a task. This plays a major role in providing an intrinsic motivation.

Consider, I am asked to make a short film on some subject. I may be knowing that subject, but may not know the art of film-making. My self-efficacy should tell me where I am strong and where I am not. If I take my weakness as a challenge, then I decide to work on it. Now I start reading about film-making out of my own interest, and not because, someone has asked me to read. This is intrinsic motivation.

If an individual –a child or an adult- has high self-efficacy, he takes reading challenge just as that—something he can master if he works diligently. Soon he becomes a good reader.

Although these two categories are stated to understand the concept of motivation for reading, in reality, a combination can be worked out. The purpose is to develop reading habit among children and adults. Therefore, it is necessary to consider a motivational mix.

c. Motivational Mix

Here is an attempt to indicate a few practical methods of self-motivation for reading. These methods are very much extrinsic in nature. But, the effect is intrinsic, thus the reader approaches the reading material based on his inner need to know more.

[These are deliberately considered as self-motivation methods. Otherwise, there is a tendency to wait for the Government to do every thing. The methods suggested here can be initiated by a parent or a teacher or a librarian or anyone, for that matter. What public library has to do is discussed elsewhere in the book. And, that is more as sustenance of reading habit.]

i. An adult with no inclination towards reading can motivate himself by attending a book talk or book discussion. Listening to a book talk does not require any special efforts from the potential reader's side. But, the net result is that his curiosity is triggered. It does so much good to develop reading habit.

ii. Reading a book may need long term attention. An uninitiated reader can not concentrate for such long hours. But, he can read book reviews. Similarly, those who are really busy also can read book reviews. They can read feature articles written about books in the weekly magazine sections of newspapers. Even reading *Reader's Digest* and other magazines is a good starting point.

iii. Seeing feature films and documentaries (*Discovery* and *National Geographic* have a number of such information products.) also help in promoting reading habits. A person who has seen movies such as *Guide, Parineeta and Devdas,* gets interested to read the books based on which these motion pictures were made. The process will generate his/her interests in the other titles by R.K Narayan and Saratchandra Chattopadhyay.

iv. Even reading newspapers properly improves reading habits. Each news or feature story is short enough to attract and hold interest of readers.

v. A recent example is the movie *3 Idiots*, and controversy between its script writers and Chetan Bhagat. The secondary reading in the press about the controversy has made more people to read Chetan Bhagat's *Five Point Someone* on which the movie is alleged to have been made. This controversy has motivated people to read the other titles too of Chetan Bagat.

In addition, one can not forget the mother of all motivation theories, Abraham Maslow's **theory of hierarchy of needs.** It is a theory in psychology, proposed by him in his 1943 paper 'A Theory of Human Motivation'. He identified five levels or hierarchies of human needs. These are given as shown below.

Level 1 : Physiological Needs. (Hunger, Thirst, Shelter, Sex etc.)

Level 2 : Security Needs

Level 3 : Social Needs: Friends, Family, Children

Level 4 : Esteem Needs, Self-Esteem, Recognition, Status

Level 5 : Self-Actualization, Creativity, Problem-Solving etc.

When a person's needs move from second to third or third to fourth or fourth to fifth levels, there is an inborn desire to read. This could be both intrinsic and extrinsic need. This can be seen from the lives of great personalities.

Lives and works of great and successful people motivate individuals -indirectly and unintentionally- to read. **To have such inspiration, it is necessary that the person receiving motivation should be ripe and mature from within. It is only then, that he/she can be receptive to these ideas.** Given below is the collage of ideas from lives and works of great people.

2.4. INSPIRATION UNLIMITED

The capacity of the human mind to unravel the mysteries of nature, apply the findings to the welfare of mankind, its imaginative power, ability to see far into the future and think deeply, are indeed not only fascinating but also supernatural and superhuman. The latest gift of these aspects of mind are the computer and the internet and other miraculous manifestations of the information technology.

With this preamble let us now see how our ancestors and their later successors, paid respect to the human mind and its desire to acquire knowledge.

XXXXX

Dr.Deepak Ranade, the noted neurosurgeon, in his article 'Human Species is so Special', argues that the frontal lobes, with which man is blessed, constitute extension of the brain and put him apart from and above his immediate ancestors - the apes. Frontal Lobes are considered as the 'Seat of Intellect'. Frontal Lobes, he avers, are "the abode of abstraction and intellect with capacity to comprehend the inner world" ("Speaking Tree", *Times of India* 23 May 2008)

It can thus be seen from these mighty references that apart from his attractive, very functional, physical form, man's intelligence, his gift of understanding and powerful memory, elevate him from other creatures and put him on a high pedestal!

The cultivation of this miracle of man's mind becomes his first and foremost duty. Neglect of this pivotal task certainly results in the man's sinking to the level of the animal world.

XXXXX

The best way to worship the God, our creator, is to make ceaseless endeavours to continuously polish our minds.

XXXXX

According to a Western statistician, for keeping our brawn i.e., physical form in fine fettle, in a span of 70 years, we taste one hundred tons of food. We utilize over 41,000 hours to munch it; and to digest it, we resort to physical exercises. But, what about the nourishment and exertion of our brains? In order to maintain the miracle of our minds, we have to seek the hospitality of educational institutions, the help of learned men and then make a beeline to their creations viz., books. We have to make sincere and severe attempts to weave into the tapestry of our lives an ardent love for reading and an enduring liking for books.

In every home, therefore, there should be a reading room and a miniature gymnasium, in addition to the dining room. Cicero (106-43 B.C.), the Roman statesman, was prophetic when he said, "A room without books is like a body without soul." Let us, therefore, pay equal attention to the upkeep and beautification of the ephemeral body as well as to the strengthening and enrichment of our eternal mind.

XXXXX

The culture of the mind, the effort to keep it ever glistening and glimmering commences from the moment the human embryo starts developing in the mother's womb. This enchanting process can be made more easy and fruitful by providing appropriate reading material to the mother after her basic traditional education. And then again we need the wisdom given by books from the moment we say, 'Thank you and Goodbye' to our educational institutions.

XXXXX

Books, as teachers, are wonderful. They are gentle and high-minded that they visit us at the place and time most convenient for us, they adjust their lessons to suit our level of intelligence and our capacity to absorb, understand and assimilate their instruction; they do not get upset if we ask them uncomfortable questions; they do not make us the butt of their jokes because of our muddle headedness; if we get bored or lose interest in their instructions, they immediately put an end to their teaching session; they come back to us and transform and elevate us into enlightened citizens with a lot of pleasure, patience, understanding, ingenuity and love. Books teach us fast and well. There is another pleasant feature about books as teachers. We do not have to pay them monthly salary, once we buy the books.

XXXXX

Sensing the crucial role that books play in keeping us enlightened and intelligent throughout our lives, Thomas Bartholin (1616-80) the physician-cum-librarian from Denmark, indulged in a hyperbole when he declared,

"Without books God is silent, Justice dormant, Science at a standstill, Philosophy lame, Literature dumb; and everything else is plunged in Cimmerian darkness."

XXXXX

The noted English poet Robert Browning (1812-1889) described books in these words.

"Books are men of higher stature
And the only men that speak louder
For further times to hear"

XXXXX

John Milton (1608-74) declared loudly, "A good book is the precious life-blood of a master-spirit, embalmed and treasured upon purpose, to a life beyond life."

XXXXX

Dr. Samuel Johnson (1709-84) English poet, critic and lexicographer, when requested by his immortal biographer James Boswell, to accompany him to attend a lecture by a dignitary quipped thus: "I cannot see that lectures can do so much good as the reading of the books from which the lectures are taken."

XXXXX

Thus, in a collection of books, we have tall men, nay, teachers of all times, all climes, all tongues and all continents.

XXXXX

Men, Who in spite of Poor Schooling, became Great by Wide and Unlimited Reading

Many of the world's tall men had no schooling or had miserably limited schooling. Most of them were born into poor families, which found it difficult to make both ends meet. They, therefore, had to work while still very young to add to their family income. And yet they strode on dauntlessly, pinching minutes and hours from their hard labour – from day break to back break, to pore over books of their interest in nearby free public libraries. Thus, embellishing their minds they blazed new trails in their chosen disciplines. Their names are a legion, but a few must be mentioned here to emphasize the point.

XXXXX

Michael Faraday (1791-1867)

Let us start with Michael Faraday, the world famous physicist and chemist in whose name a universally acclaimed research society has been established in London. Young Michael was one of the several children of a London blacksmith. At the age of 10 or so when he finished his free elementary education, he was, at the entreaty of his father, hired by Ribou, owner of a secondhand book shop in London, as a helper to his binder. The bindery was located in the basement of the shop with no electricity and central heating. Poor Michael slogged on in candle light and during his spare time, was absorbed in studying and taking down notes from worn out books in physics and chemistry, which came in for repairs and binding. Being a precocious child, he soon gained considerable knowledge in these subjects and caught the attention of a member of the Chemistry Faculty of the Cambridge University, who had come to buy old books. Result: he soon joined the Chemistry Department in the University, as a bottle washer. And this small opening paved the way for him to ascend later the Chair of Professor of Chemistry (1833), which had been adorned by Sir Humphry Davy. The dingy bindery – the chemistry lab became his College and University. Faraday's name is firmly associated with electricity and electro-chemistry.

XXXXX

Benjamin Franklin (1706-1790)

Born into a family of very humble means young Benjamin had to work in a printing press to supplement the meager resources of his parents. During his leisure time in the press he would, with devotion, study the books being printed. In this way he gleaned and garnered knowledge, later to become a scientist and a diplomat. His then future wife, Deborah Reed used to see him in front of her house walking along the road in Philadelphia, eating a loaf of bread bought by him, paying his last penny.

Franklin invented the lightening conductor, became Deputy Postmaster of Philadelphia and later as a member of the Continental Congress, helped Thomas Jefferson, the third President (1801-09) of the USA to draft the famous 'Declaration of Independence' (4 July 1776).

He used to say, **"No man can be truly educated in life, unless he is a reader of books."**

XXXXX

Thomas Alva Edison (1847-1931)

Unable to continue his education, after the elementary stage, young Edison sold newspapers at the railway station at train times. During the interval between two trains, he would make a beeline to the near by Detroit Public Library to collect and store ideas from books of his choice. He is hailed probably as the most prolific scientific inventor. Gradually he built up his own research laboratory in Menlo Park, New Jersey. His inventions number over 1300 and include the electric bulb, gramophone etc. Edison had set up a generating unit, which supplied electricity to over 80 customers!

XXXXX

Abraham Lincoln (1809-1865)

Emancipator of Negro slaves in the USA, Abraham was born in a log cabin, son of a carpenter, who recklessly squandered his meager earnings. As a young lad Abraham had to split wood and remove husk from corn from early in the morning till late at night. He would then start his studies. Since he could not buy slate or paper, he would use pieces of wood and charcoal for writing. He used to tell his friends, "The things I want to know are in books. My best friend is the man who will give me a book." It is said that on one occasion he walked 40 miles to borrow a book!

XXXXX

Napoleon Bonaparte I - Emperor of France (1769 – 1821)

As a young lad he was sent to the military school. When he turned 14, he found his number according to merit in the class was 42, which meant, 41 boys were ahead of him in studies. Later when he joined the army as an Officer, he slept only for five hours and devoted most of his spare time for reading. His secretary sent him a constant stream of a grand variety of books. Result: None of the 41 boys, who were above him, is remembered today!

XXXXX

Andrew Carnegie (1835-1919)

Son of a poor weaver in Scotland, Andrew migrated to the USA – Pittsburgh – along with his parents at the age of 12, to escape poverty. Starting his working life as a 'Bobbin boy', he soon secured a job as a messenger in a telegraph office. During his spare time he read books borrowed from a small public library established by Colonel Anderson, especially for poor boys and girls like Andrew.

He soon joined the Pennsylvania Rail Road Company. His learning, audacity and adroitness attracted the attention of Theodore W^odruff of the Sleeping Car Company, who enrolled him as a shareholder. Andrew soon was involved in railroads and steel production.

As a wealthy man he published a paper 'Gospel of Wealth' which was widely read. He advocated that the wealthy should lead a simple life and donate their savings for philanthropy; himself setting a noble example by establishing 2500 free public libraries in the English speaking world.

Later he paid a grateful tribute to Colonel Anderson in these words:

"...This is but a light tribute and gives only a faint idea of the depth of gratitude, which I feel for what he did for me and my companions. It was from my own early experience that I decided there was no use to which money could be applied so productive of good boys and girls who have good within them and ability and ambition to develop it, as the founding of a public library in a community."

XXXXX

Alfred E Smith – Governor of New York (1873-1944)

As a lad of 14, Alfred sold fish in Fulton Street Fish Market (F.F.M.) in New York to add to his parents' severely limited income. He saved money and bought books; the reading of these transported him from his ugly environment. He sculpted himself into eminence and soon rose to be the Governor of New York. After one of his cabinet meetings, one day, the members while waiting for tea and snacks to arrive, started reminiscing about their college days, with Smith quietly enjoying their chatter rather attentively. At last one of his cabinet members turned to him and said "May it please your Excellency! It is now your turn to tell us which great institution had the privilege of having your Excellency as its worthy alumnus." In reply Smith said jokingly, "Well, dear folks, I am an old graduate of FFM". The members were taken aback, for they had never heard of such a Center of higher learning anywhere in the world. Smith continued and declared, "Books alone were my teachers, my library, my alma mater."

XXXXX

Helen Keller Adams (1880-1968)

Blind and deaf, through a cruel illness when she was just 19 months old, she yet learned to read and write and finally graduated from Radclliffe College, Cambridge, (Massachusetts, USA). Through books – "those magic springs of healing and refreshment, she found more to make life worthwhile than many others, who have eyes and ears, but never learned to employ the faculties of the head and heart."

XXXXX

John Masefield (1878 – 1967)

Born poor, he had to work as a porter in New York harbour; but bought books from his savings and devotedly studied them. Geoffrey Chaucer's (1342-1400) *Parliament of Fowls* deeply stirred him, and he vowed to become a poet. He was elevated to poet laureateship in 1930.

XXXXX

Arthur Kavanagh (1831-1889)

Irish politician born with mere rudiments of arms and legs, yet learned to read and write holding a pen in his teeth.

Later he learnt riding horse and to shoot. He came to India and worked in the Land Records Department. A discriminating reader, he was Member of British Parliament for 12 years.

XXXXX

David Lloyd George (1863-1945)

As a young boy he worked in the cobbler's shop owned and operated by his uncle. His teachers - good learned books borrowed from friends and public libraries- enabled him to be a powerful speaker and enter Parliament in 1890. He was Prime Minister of Great Britain for eight years from 1914-1922.

XXXXX

Rabindranath Tagore (1861-1941)

Unlike all the other eminent men mentioned above, Rabindranath was born with a golden spoon in his mouth. He was sent to the best schools in Calcutta but the young lad, found them 'inhospitable'. Finally, the parents thought of hiring a teacher who would come to their palatial bungalow to tutor their child. Even this he resented.

But the atmosphere at home was highly cultured. There was a grand home library. His eldest sister was a Sanskrit scholar, one of his elder brothers was a District Judge, having passed his ICS (he served as District Judge in Karwar, Karnataka), and yet another one, was an eminent painter. Growing up amidst books and such highly enlightened surroundings Tagore bloomed as a notable very young poet - a child prodigy, when he had crossed the threshold of his 13th year. Later he was crowned with the Nobel Prize for his *Geetanjali* in 1913.

XXXXX

SOME GREAT LOVERS OF BOOKS

Sir C.V.Raman (1880-1970)

In a symposium titled, *Books That Have Influenced Me*, published in 1947 by the famous publisher of Madras (now Chennai) - G.A.Natesan & Co., Sir C.V.Raman writes *inter alia*,

"The copy of *Kidnapped* I had purchased and used disappeared. In due course, one evening, a couple of years ago, a copy of Robert Louis Stevenson's (1850-94) *Kidnapped*, beautifully printed and bound, caught my eye at a railway book stall. I was tempted to buy it and started reading the book before going to bed. Believe it or not, the story or rather the manner in its telling gripped me so powerfully, that I had finished reading the book at one sitting, before resting for the night. Since then I have read everything that Stevenson wrote with the keenest enjoyment. Indeed a good home and a good school may be judged by the kind of books they put in the way of a growing young person for him to feed his mind and his emotions upon."

Later he read Sir Edwin Arnold's *Light of Asia*, and was powerfully moved by the story of Siddhartha's renunciation.

Referring to the drawbacks of the system of prescribing textbooks, Sir C.V. remarked, "The element of compulsion, introduced in the prescription of books for study, is usually fatal to that attitude of mind, which is necessary for the full appreciation of their contents."

XXXXX

Sri Aurobindo (1872-1950)

Sri Aurobindo, Jawaharlal Nehru, Dr.Babasaheb Ambedkar, to name a few of our tall men, were great lovers of books. Sri Aurobindo, first as a professor of Maharaja's College at Baroda and later as its Principal, spent a lion's share of his salary on buying books!

XXXXX

Jawaharlal Nehru (1889 - 1964)

Jawaharlal Nehru - as Prime Minister slogged for 18 hours a day, and yet found time, before going to bed to pore over a new book, that he may have chanced to come by. A few days, prior to his passing away, somebody placed in his hands Robert Frost's latest collection of poems. Nehru went through it assiduously, liked one of the poems titled "Stopping by Woods on a Snowy Evening" very much, copied the following lines from it and placed the slip of paper below the glass top on his table. The lines, which probably evoked his emotions, ran like this:

"The woods are lovely dark and deep
But I have promises to keep
And miles to go before I sleep
And miles to go before I sleep"

Besides being an enthralling orator, Nehru was a charming writer. His autobiography was reprinted nine times in 1936 and witnessed 16 reprints in 10 years. His gift to the world -"Better History and Beautiful English."

But for his love of books and learning and that of Shri. C. Rajagopalachari of hallowed memory, the Belvedere palace in Kolkata, would never have been the lovely abode of our National Library.

XXXXX

Dr. B.R.Ambedkar (1894 – 1956)

A beautiful anecdote is told about Dr.Ambedkar's fascination for books. Having established the Siddhartha College in Mumbai, Dr.Ambedkar wanted the College Library to be very rich. He appointed Mr. S. S. Rege, a great connoisseur of books, particularly rare ones, as Librarian. From day one of his appointment Rege exceeded the budget provision for buying choice books and it became a habit with him. This over enthusiasm for good books on his part, led Rege to cross all allocation limits on one occasion. The budget provision for the Library was a few thousand rupees, but he had committed the Institution to a lakh and more. Naturally the Registrar and the Finance Officer took an unfavourable view of it. The agenda for a special meeting of the College Executive Committee included this item. Every body in the College felt that Dr.Ambedkar would probably ask Mr.Rege to be more cautious in future. The meeting day arrived. Dr.Ambedkar came on time to preside over the meeting. As was his wont, he first went to the College Library and inspected the exhibition of the newly acquired books and then to the meeting hall. When Mr Rege's item came for discussion, Dr.Ambedkar coolly approved the excess expenditure and asked the Finance Officer to enhance the book grant by a few thousand rupees for purchase of rare books by Mr Rege.

XXXXX

Dr. K. V. Puttappa (KUVEMPU) (1904 - 1994)

Kuppali Venkatappagowda Puttappa (December 29, 1904 - November 11, 1994) was a well-known Kannada writer and a poet. He is the first among the seven recipients of Jnanpith award for Kannada. Puttappa wrote all his literary works using the pen-name *Kuvempu.*

Kuvempu came to Mysore to continue his education in high school and college after completing his primary education in his native village. One day in the evening he chanced by the Mysore City Central Library housed in a beautiful heritage edifice. He gazed in wonder and awe at the tall shelves, studded with beautiful books through the windowpanes. The electric lamp chandeliers, with a garland of electric bulbs, lent enchantment to the sight. At once his innate urge to read and prosper got immensely whetted. Later through the courtesy of a classmate, with appropriate contacts in the city, he visited the Library and grew lyrical about his impressions of the inside of the Library among the mighty minds of all times, of all climes and of all tongues. Listen to his effusive eloquence on the majestic effect the collection relating to Sri Ramakrishna Paramahamsa and Swamy Vivekananda made on him. "As I stood gazing in wonder, my eyes were greeted by the blessed collection of books by the Divine Sri Ramakrishna Paramahamsa and Swamy Vivekananda, which eternally changed the orientation of my life and transposed me from this humdrum work a day world into the haven of bliss." (Kuvempu: *Nenapina Doniyalli.* Vol. 1 p.125-128.)

XXXXX

Dr. V. K. Gokak (1909 – 1992)

Dr.Gokak was the fifth of the seven recipients of Jnanpith award in Kannada language. a brilliant student of the famous Karnataka College, (Dharwad) obtained his Bachelor's and Master's degrees with English literature with distinction from the University of Bombay, and was immediately appointed as Professor of English in Ferguson College in Pune. His classmates and colleagues marveled at his amazing oratory.

His desire for earning more knowledge, almost supremacy in his chosen subject, propelled him into seeking the hospitality of the Oxford University, which proudly claimed that it had universally acclaimed Professors in English literature and a scholarly collection in its world famous Bodleian Library (1409).

He obtained a huge loan to cover his travel, stay expenses and fees etc in Oxford and enrolled for the BA degree class! (Oxford, in those days did not have any regular M.A. classes. Students who had passed their Bachelor's degree could, if they so desired, obtain the M.A. degree certificate, after a couple of years by paying the requisite fee.) From the day he landed in Oxford till the date of his exam, he spent most of his waking hours reading in the Library, in attending lectures and in discussing with his professors.

The day of viva (after he had appeared for the theory papers) arrived. But suddenly he started having excruciating pain in his stomach. The doctor who was immediately consulted opined that it was a bad attack of appendicitis and that Gokak had to be immediately operated upon. So instead of the exam hall, young Gokak was admitted into the hospital!

By the time he was discharged from the hospital, the viva was over. And yet he was declared to have passed the exam in the first class, thanks to his love of books! The essays he had submitted during the year were indeed of a high quality warranting a first class in the exams.

XXXXX

Dr (Smt) Sudha Murthy

In these days of the glitter, glamour and glory of the Internet, when there is loud talk of paperless society, libraries without walls and the sounding of the death-knell of the conventional book by the marvels of IT, it is heartening to find a rare, incomparable icon of the Internet world, panegyrizing (speaking in praise) about the central role which books play in our lives. Listen to Dr. (Smt) Sudha Murthy, Chairperson of the Infosys Foundation, paying tributes eloquently to books/libraries and reading:

"I feel libraries play an important role in the lives of children, the citizens of tomorrow. As I was raised in a middle class family in a small rural town, I was well aware of the importance of books and knowledge in the life of a student. Those were also the days when I had limited access to books and actually it was then that I envisaged a free of cost unlimited access to library. And as soon as I was named trustee of the Foundation, I knew I had to take the first steps towards fulfilling my desire of building libraries for village children.

Reading has many advantages. It is not only a useful hobby, but also helps us imbibe better qualities of the mind. Keeping this in mind, the Trustees planned at establishing libraries that comprised books in regional language and not textbooks that the children were studying in schools. Simple illustrated interesting books that could be read without anybody's help were thus selected for these libraries."

Infosys has established, under its 'A Library for Each Village Project', 4000 village libraries so far, and the programme is still going on.

Recently, the Foundation has provided libraries to 700 villages of coastal Karnataka, in collaboration with an NGO - Shri Kshetra Dharmasthala Rural Development Project. The beneficiaries of these libraries will be rural women. (Sudha Murthy 2002. *Wise and Otherwise*. 2002. p40-44)

XXXXX

Sri Ranga - Adya Rangacharya

Sri Ranga - founder of the modern drama in Kannada (formerly Prof. R. V. Jahagirdar - Professor of Sanskrit, Karnataka College, Dharwad) was a voracious reader as a young lad. By the time he attained his 14th year, he had memorized the whole of *Amar Kosha* and large parts of *Mahabharat* which runs, into over 1,00,000 verses. He and his friends, while studying in a high school in Bijapur, were fascinated by the novels of the 'Father of Kannada Novels' Sri Galaganath, which were being serialized in the popular Kannada monthly *Sadbodha Chandrike*. They took out a common subscription for it and on the expected day of the arrival of the issues, they used to rush to the post office, tip the postman to get their issue on priority - and then start reading beneath a nearby shady tree. Sri Ranga bloomed into a great orator and was spontaneous in repartee and a brilliant trail blazer in modern Kannada drama.

XXXXX

Michaelangelo Bounarotti (1475 – 1564)

One last example of a person who was learning from books in his late eighties is that of Michelangelo, Italian sculptor painter, architect and poet. When a friend who called on him during his last days asked him why he was reading, his characteristic reply was "*Ancora Impara*", which means, "still learning."

XXXXX

After this illustrative collage about what reading has done to great personalities, it is time to consolidate on how reading helps the reader.

2.5. BENEFITS OF READING

Art being long and life being short, we should invest all our leisure hours in meaningful fruitful activities, like physical exercises for the body, because it is the temple of our Divinity, and has to be kept in shipshape always, and reading and discussions with the learned, which are the appropriate exercises for our minds which are considered the presiding deities of the body.

Time is more than money; and in this valuable raw material we are all equally rich. Michael Faraday had very early in life realized the value and importance of time. In a letter to one of his friends he wrote, "Time is all I ask for; time is all I require. Oh! That I could purchase, at a cheap rate, some of our modern gents' spare hours, nay days, I think it would be a good bargain to both, for them and me."

William Evart Gladstone (1809-98) four times Prime Minister of Great Britain, always carried a book in his coat pocket. Result: His mind was at its best when he was 85. An

American magazine requested him to write articles for it at the rate of $ 1.00 for every word.

a. Urge to Read, Write and be Educated

The urge to read, write and pass off as educated persons lies hidden in the human heart, because of the fact that man is blessed with the gift of mind. And for this impulse to find fruition facilities such as schools and libraries have to be provided in ample and easy measure by the society.

When the Unesco, immediately after it was ushered into being, sponsored its fundamental programmes viz., 'Education For All' and 'Books For All', a very revealing incident emerged from a developing country in the continent of Africa.

This country, which received aid from the Unesco to implement the above programmes, used a portion of the funds for buying a large quantity of tops of pens - note, it was only tops of pens- from a developed country. Reason for this curious transaction was that, a great majority of the people of that country were illiterate, yet they wanted to show off to others that they were educated by flaunting the tops of pens in the outer pockets of their coats and jackets!

At least, they knew that it is important to be educated! Even those who were not literate knew the importance of being and projecting themselves as literates!

b. Influence of Reading

Books besides serving mankind as educators also have the influence to change the course of the lives of individuals, and even the direction of the histories of nations. Books are power, because of the influence -socially, politically and in any other sense- they have on us.

Such books are a legion; but for our present purpose, however a few are being referred to in passing, while the impact of one, which is of interest, is described in some detail.

i. Barrack Obama, an African American of mixed parentage, secured a thumping majority at the Presidential Election and strode into the White House with a lot of fanfare, music, colour and gold! (As a young boy when he went to a white hotel and asked for a cup of tea he was refused.) How did this miracle of centuries unravel itself now?

The seeds of this wonder of wonders go back to the 1850's when Negro slavery was rampaging in the US. Young adventurous white Americans, sought the hospitality of the shores of the Dark Continent, with not any noble intention, but with the evil, poisonous motive of chasing and catching young negroes, chaining them and transporting them in ships across the oceans to the shores of USA; and there to sell them like cattle, items of furniture to the rich land owners of the southern states. These land owners needed young blacks as slaves to work on their expansive fields. The young blacks toiled from day break to back break, and any slackness or indifference on their part, was visited with beatings, black & blue, from their white masters!

The spark or the trigger of change came in the form of Harriet Beecher Stowe. She was a young white woman with a highly spiritual and religious background. She saw these ugly, most cruel happenings in her neighborhood and was mightily moved with candid compassion for the eternally suffering blacks. At night over dinner, she would relate to her near and dear ties, the heart rending happenings she saw in the course of the day. Her sister-in-law, Mrs. Edward Beecher, implored Harriet to write something that would make a whole nation feel what an accursed thing slavery was.

Result – the script of the beautiful but blood-curdling novel, *Uncle Tom's Cabin* was soon ready. The Editor of *National Era* mustered courage, in both his hands and launched upon the adventure of publishing the novel in the serial form from June 1851. The gruesome story so caught the imagination of the Northerners that a small publishing firm in Boston, published the novel in two volumes.

The first edition was in 5000 copies of which 3000 were sold on the first day and the balance went the next day. Orders poured in and 300,000 copies were sold by the end of the year. Eight power presses were running night and day to meet the demand and three paper mills were supplying the paper.

Abraham Lincoln was so powerfully influenced by the book that he issued the "Proclamation Emancipating the Slaves." Charles Sumner a noted critic had this to say "If *Uncle Tom's Cabin* had not been written, Lincoln would not have been elected President of the USA."

When Harriet called on Lincoln at the White House he greeted with these words, "The little lady who wrote the book that made the big war." (civil war).

ii. John Ruskin (1819-1900)'s little book *Unto This Last* transformed the then a struggling barrister Mr. M. K. Gandhi, in South Africa, into the Mighty Mahatma Gandhi.

iii. Romain Rolland (1866 – 1941)'s biography of Mahatma Gandhi made Madeleine Slade (1892–1902), daughter of the British Navy Chief, Admiral Slade, into turning her back upon a life of luxury and ease, of pomp and pleasure, a life full of the glimmer of pearls and gloss of satin, and adopting the hard life of the *satyagrahi* of Sabarmati Ashram in Ahemdabad.

iv. E. Stanley Jones' *Mahatma Gandhi An Interpretation* (1948), so powerfully influenced Martin Luther King (Jr.) (1929-68) that he whole-heartedly adopted the eternal principle of nonviolence with love, and was soon hailed as the Gandhi of the USA. In his famous poetical address delivered on the steps of the Lincoln Memorial on 28 August 1963, entitled 'I have a Dream', he boldly prophesied thus, "America will soon wake up and implement fully the universal law that all men are created equal." For advocating such liberal views, he was assassinated in 1968; but his noble dream has come true and black Barrack Obama now presides over the destiny of the USA – the most powerful and rich nation in the world.

v. Louis Fischer's *Life of Mahatma Gandhi* bewitched Lord Attenbourough into launching upon the adventure of making a memorable Oscar winning film on Gandhi.

vi. Karl Marx (1818 – 1883)'s *Das Kapital* brought cheer into the lives of labourers all over the world.

vii. Thomas R Malthus's (1766-1834) *Essay on the Principle of Population*, led to the establishment of Family Welfare Associations throughout the World.

viii. J.K.Rowling's *Harry Potter* volumes have captured the imagination of children all over the world. Over 400 million copies have been sold so far. Next to the British Queen, Rowling has bloomed into the richest woman in Britain with £ 545 million royalty in her bank account.

This is just a glimpse of the influence of reading in general and books in particular.

c. Books have the power to heal us too – Bibliotherapy

Books have a curative effect on our diseases also. Aulus Cornelius Celsus (1st century AD), Roman scholar, compiled an Encyclopedia, of which *De Medicina* part only has survived. In this part, Celsus has highlighted the curative effects of reading on certain of our ailments.

Robert Burton (1577–1640), a British scholar, completed and published his *Anatomy of Melancholy*, which describes in detail how reading helps in banishing several bodily diseases.

Men of medicine all over the world have been prescribing appropriate reading as a panacea. Several hospitals have established good libraries for the purpose. Light literature - humorous stories, dramas etc., classics like *Ramayana,* classical as well light music cassettes, are being prescribed to lift up drooping souls, calm agitated minds, and instill hope and the spirit of joy and enthusiasm among patients.

John Florio, an Italian writer, who taught at the Oxford University, haa this to say about the healthy effect reading has on patients. "**Reading is the best medicine for a sick man, the best music for a sad man, the best counsel for a desperate man, the best comfort for one afflicted.**"

The Webster's New International Dictionary included for the first time, the word Bibliotherapy in 1961. The meaning of the term it gave runs thus: "The use of selected reading materials as therapeutic adjutants in medicine and psychiatry; guidance in the solution of personal problems through directed reading."

Hospital librarians have to get special training in this area. The journal *Library Trends* devoted a whole issue (No.2, October 1962) to discuss threadbare the various aspects of the therapy.

e. Entertainment Value of Books

We read books - humorous, light ones to entertain ourselves, to banish our boredom and also when in tours and travels.

The system of reading out books, extracts from classics, to both literate and illiterate groups is still in vogue in rural and religious circles. Temples and *Maths* organize such programmes at the time of festivals. Such sessions are indeed educative, besides being enlightening.

A unique example of this useful and even ennobling system which has gone into the history of English literature is that of Samuel Richardson(1689 -1761)'s, pioneering novel *Pamela* (1740).

Richardson was unique exception to his times of loose morals. He was a strict moralist, a rigid teetotaler and a pure vegetarian. The novel runs into over 600 pages and is in the form of letters. At Slough, a village in Berkshire, England, on the request of the villagers, the village blacksmith used to read out the novel every night by the forge fire. This went on for over a few months.

Pamela, the heroine who loved a young man, had to pass through several ordeals before she could realize her ambition. When on the last day of the reading, Pamela got married to her young lover, it was past midnight. But the villagers were so joyous and excited that their heroine was happily married, they rose in a mass, marched to the village church, woke up the presiding priest, and requested him to ring the church bell to celebrate the marriage! (Compton-Rickett, Arthur: *History of English Literature*. P247.)

A lifelong study is enjoined upon us by the great champion of English literature - Dr.Samuel Johnson, at whose feet, the mightiest of his times - Edmund Burke, the orator, Goldsmith, the poet, Reynolds the painter, Garrick the actor, Gibbon, the historian, all sat in the coffeehouse and in addition to consuming coffee, drank from the fountain of his vast knowledge. Dr.Johnson declared thus heightening the importance of reading,

"Those who do not read can have nothing to think and little to say." Well, nothing more needs to be said regarding importance of reading.

The process of motivating potential readers -young or old- is successful if and only if people read because they want to, and not because they have to. That is the essence of motivation.

3

CHILDREN AND READING

Every parent wishes that his/her child should become a scholar and a successful personality. For this, they want the kids to read more and become more knowledgeable. But, they seldom realize what is happening to the child, how it is developing in relation to reading and acquiring knowledge. [Of course, those who have studied developmental psychology know it. But, a common man has to depend only on his/her common sense.]

It is a common observation that a child is better in reading and writing in its mother tongue than in any other languages. But why is it?

There are four language related skills, viz., listening, speaking, writing and reading. A child learns mother tongue in this order. But, in case of second and third languages, we first learn to write, then to read followed by speaking. Listening is interwoven in all these skills. Even if second and third languages can be acquainted in the order in which mother tongue is learned, one can get better command. [I can speak Tamil because I lived in Chennai for 16 years. But I can not read and write that language. But, if I now make an attempt, I will pick up the reading and writing skill faster.]

Language skills are better picked up in childhood than after growing up. Dr.Max Cynaber, a University of British Columbia Neurosurgeon points out that a person is born with learning ability; but if he is **not stimulated or educated before he is two years old, one third (1/3) of the outer brain cells will surely die!**

3.1. READING BEFORE READING

It is found that at 18 months of age, a child adds one word to its vocabulary in every two hours. By the time a child is of two years, it knows over 2000 words, and can construct sentences with two words. 'I want', 'Don't go' etc. By three years, a child gets grammar rules regarding tense and number.

Children learn the reading process much before they identify the alphabets. Amazing, but it is true. The following are a few aspects of child development which point at this phenomenon.

- When they make a pattern with objects such as buttons, beads, colored cubes, they are learning about the sequence. This helps them in understanding the order of alphabets in words and subsequently, words in a sentence.
- Listening to stories and telling them to their parents and friends develop concepts about time, place and people.
- Story telling teaches them to understand beginning, middle and end of communication.
- When their parents or teachers are reading stories loudly, they learn that spoken words can be written down, can be printed and can again be converted into spoken words in the process of reading.

- Posters and advertisements with biscuits, chocolates, cars etc. give them the idea that print and written medium provide information.
- The concepts of directions like up, down, left and right, leads to reading from left to right and from top to bottom.
- Playing with papers and books -particularly picture books, they learn that on every page there is something new to be seen. With this they learn to turn pages. (Source : *http://www.readingrockets.org/article/386*)

A child does not pick up these skills for the sake of reading. Even an illiterate or a tribal person has these skills. But, reading is based on these skills. Well, anyway the child acquires the foundation of reading skills, and thus receives indirect motivation without its conscious effort.

While a child is getting ready to read even before it learns to identify alphabets, the world outside also should make necessary efforts to develop and sustain reading habits.

While there is conducive environment for developing reading habit in the advanced countries, in India and other third world nations the situation is grim. The movement for making books dear and near to children has spread in Great Britain, Netherlands, and it has spread even to China. In these countries it is said, high-school students too are buying books, from their pocket money.

In our country, even basic amenities are not available to children. The needs of children -physical, emotional and intellectual- have to be met on a top priority basis. Unfortunately, in our country children continue to receive scant attention. The plight of girl children is much worse.

A quick, cursory glance at the plight of our primary schools will drive home this fact. This is a dangerous trend and ultimately hurts our own future. Our own security and happiness lies firmly in children's hands. We must pay heed to the warning given to us by Madame Gabriele Mistratl (1889-1957) the Nobel Prize winner poetess of Chile; this is how she cautions us:

"We are guilty of many errors and many faults; but our worst crime is abandoning the children, neglecting the fountain of our life. Many of the things we need can wait. The child cannot. Right now is the time his bones are being formed, his blood is being made and his senses are being developed. To him we cannot answer 'Tomorrow'. His name is 'Today'."

This is both a macro and micro problem. Concern about children at macro level, include infant mortality, malnutrition, family health, child abuse, education etc. Even, if we focus only on reading habit, there are many things the Government has to do. That is a long drawn process. Let us focus on what we can do at our end. If child has learned to read before identifying alphabets, how should parents develop reading habits in children?

3.2. READING HABIT IN CHILDREN

Children love reading, they like books. But the habit should not be lost in the process of growing. Children have to be motivated at this delicate age. Some select ideas are presented here.

i. Children should be introduced to books even before preschool days. They should be given books and audio-visual material in the form of CDs and VCDs. Kids should be given books as gifts. They should develop the habit of sharing books with other children.

ii. Books should be read aloud to children by parents. They should be shown the pictures, taught to identify animal characters and individual roles of the story books. Kids should be encouraged to tell the stories.

iii. Children should be taken to libraries, bookshops and book-fairs. They should be shown Internet Public Library's site. (*http://www.ipl.org/*), particularly, 'kidspace' and 'teenspace' within the site. There are many such sites on the net.

iv. They should also be taken to zoos, flower and fruits exhibitions, museums and planetariums. This helps them to associate or relate books and their contents to the world around. In short, reading is to be introduced as one way of exploring the surrounding world/ nature.

v. As a child grows, the visual content in the books reduces; font size becomes smaller. The subject also becomes more abstract. This is the time when child may start losing interest in reading. Special attention should be given at this stage.

Children should be prepared to face this change in the reading materials. But, how to achieve it? Perhaps, this should be done just as a growing kid is introduced to the idea of the arrival of the second child in the family. Child is generally asked if it needs someone to play with. After getting an affirmation, we tell him/her that you will now be an elder brother/sister. Gradually make the kid to look forward to the arrival of the second child. Such efforts help in reducing sibling rivalry among growing children.

Similarly, we must show them the books we read and point out that there are no pictures in them. Also, bring it to the child's notice that we do not read loudly, nor do we make any lip movement while reading. Tell the kid about content of some of the books we read in simple language. Let the kid understand that he should expect and welcome the change.

These are some easy-to-follow tips to motivate kids to read.

Once the reading habit is developed, then it has to be sustained. It is nice to see auto-rickshaw, taxi drivers, cycle-rickshaw pullers, vegetable vendors, fishermen in Kerala buying, carrying and reading newspapers. Once the habit is formed, what matters is what to read and when.

4

What to Read and When to Read

Even when a child or an adult is highly motivated to read, it is difficult to develop and sustain reading habit. Being motivated to read is one thing and developing and sustaining the habit is another. It needs a catalyst. The habit is reinforced by reading what interests him/her. Forcing a teenager to study spiritual books may repel the child from reading. Therefore, knowing what to read and when is very important.

In an ideal condition it appears that these are two stupid questions. The '**ideal**' answers for these questions are given below.

- The ideal answer to the first question should be that anything and everything should be read. Each book is unique. It has its own purpose. It addresses to a specific target group of readers. Professor Ranganathan, puts it as the third law of library science, "Every book its reader." However specific the subject matter may be, even a novice may take interest in a book, if it is not too technical or mathematical in its treatment.

Thus, as a librarian blogger says, there are no bad books, only badly written ones. **Aldous Huxley** says, "A bad book is as much of a labor to write as a good one, it comes as sincerely from the author's soul." [Source: *Point Counter Point*, 1928. Ch. 13. Thus, all books are good books. Hence, in principle, all books are worth reading.

- The ideal answer to the second question, in principle, should be that one can and should read anytime possible and 24 X 7.

The above two are ideal, desirable and dogmatic, but not possible.

First, it is humanly impossible for anyone to read all the books, all the time. Reading is not the only thing we do or we should be doing. One needs to do some work to earn his/her bread. One has to commute to and from workplace. There are physiological needs such as sleep, food, bath etc. There is need to reflect and to attend to many other responsibilities of life. After all, one needs to apply and reflect what is read.

This means we have to select and prioritise what is to be read. This is the essence of reading habit.

During my 16 years of working life at the British Council Library, Madras (Chennai), I came across many voracious readers. They all were senior professionals, professors, doctors, engineers and civil servants. In short, they were either well brought up or self-made individuals. I was amazed by their reading habits. The variety of books they used to ask for and read made me interested in knowing how they developed such intense reading habit. I had many questions for such readers. I was curious to know,

i. What they used to read as children and when?

ii. How their choice of reading evolved? What makes them choose a particular book?

iii. Why do they read?

iv. How they used to find time for reading?

v. How do they read so much?

vi. Do they comprehend everything they read?

vii. How do they remember the essence of what they read when they want?

Since, I had developed a very warm relationship with most of the readers, I could ask them directly. No single reader was asked all the seven questions at a time. It was not intended to be any rigorous research work. I was only driven by my curiosity at that time. Today I can look back and consolidate the responses received from different readers at different occasions along with my own reading and observations. These inputs give a pattern which points at some guidelines.

The guidelines emerging from the first two questions are listed in this chapter under the sections, 'Evolution of Reading Habit' and 'A Tentative Plan for Reading'. The third question will be covered in the next and last three in the following two chapters.

4.1. EVOLUTION OF READING HABIT

Children are inducted to reading habit due to the encouragement given by their parents or some teacher or a childhood role model and due to their inner curiosity to know the world around. Reading habit has to be evolved gradually as part of growing up process.

A child should be introduced to picture books in preschool years. Cartoon films have a great role in holding and retaining their interest in reading. Then comics etc. are ideal between 6-10 years of age. This is the age when stories should be read out loudly to them. They should be asked to narrate the stories told to them.

Between 8 - 12 years of age, children start reading comics (stories) of Phantom, Mandrake etc. Panchatantra stories, Aesop's Fables interest kids. Initially they love to listen to these stories, then to read in the form of comics. These are the years when a child is growing from fantasy to reality. Gradually they lose interest in such books with animals, princes, princesses, magic carpets, demons, *Rishis* etc. They need something more concrete and holding their interest and triggering their imagination in their teen years. These are the years of transition.

What to read at this stage is very crucial. Therefore, it is necessary to draw some broad guidelines regarding what to read and when. The choice and timing of reading has to depend on the age of the reader.

The following are a few ideal reading materials in early teen years. These are presented in the following three stages.

Stage 1 : The ideal starters are short stories. As children have limited span of interest, they can finish reading quickly. Preferably they should start reading stories they already know. These stories deal with folk and mythological characters.

Stories from *Ramayana* and *Mahabharata* are very good for Indian kids. Consider stories of Shravankumar, Bharat and Rama, Hanuman and how he burnt Lanka, Bakasura, Eklavya, Arjuna as Brihannala are very ideal in holding children's interest.

Chacha Chaudhary, Mulla Nasruddin stories help in developing intelligence in children.

Arabian Nights is the English version of *One Thousand and One Nights.* It is a collection of 1001 folk tales intertwined into a single story. Some of the best-known tales such as *Aladdin's Wonder Lamp, Ali Baba and the Forty Thieves* and *Seven Voyages of Sindabad* have been included in the Arabian Nights translated by Antoine Galland and other European translators. But, these were not parts of the original Arabic version.

Vikram-Betal is also a collection of intertwined stories. Like *Arabian Nights*, one story leads to another. Although all these are packaged into one story, each one can be read and enjoyed independently.

Similarly stories of Cinderella, Robin Hood, Robinson Crusoe, William Tell are necessary for introducing them to the world literature. These stories in comic form or five to ten page stories makes good reading.

Stage 2 : This is the stage the child is between 12 to 15 years of age. The stories liked by them no longer deal with just folk or mythological characters. The characters start appearing real and authentic. The characters either represent those individuals who once lived on this Earth (eg: Akbar, Tenali Ram etc.) or the leading characters in the tales are boys and girls of the readers' age. This helps to develop an identity with the characters.

Akbar-Birbal stories are of great interest to kids at this stage. Similarly, Tenali Ram's stories and R.K. Narayan' *Swami and Friends, Malgudi Days* help children to gradually increase the reading habit.

The next step is to read Ruskin Bond's stories. [Or similar stories.]

Enid Blyton also known as Mary Pollock's books are very popular among children, particularly girls.

The Hardy Boys, Frank and Joe Hardy are fictional characters. They are teenage brothers. Their stories deal with mysteries where the boys are amateur detectives. These stories are very popular. These stories are written by different ghost writers over years under pseudonym Franklyn Dixon.

Stage 3 : This is when the child is in 16 to 19 years age group. In a popular lecture Mr M.V. Kamat, the famous journalist, said that he developed his reading habit by starting on Agatha Christie's detective fictions. Yes, detective stories are ideal starting point to get into the world literature, as these hold the readers' interest. The reader gets so much absorbed in reading detective fictions/ crime stories that he/ she would like to finish it in one sitting.

Short stories of William **Somerset Maugham, O. Henry** [It is pseudonym of the American writer William Sydney Porter.] are excellent to read. These stories help a reader in graduating to serious literature.

Similarly, plays have a great role in developing reading habit. The best aspect of plays is that it is in the form of dialogues/conversations. The lines are short, crisp and direct. It is easy and interesting to read humorous or mythological plays. At this stage reading is to widen horizon, for recreation and even for developing the habit of reading. The reading habit is still evolving. There are three aspects of further development of reading habit of the growing individual at this stage.

Stage 3A: Introduction to Classics : As Prof. K. S. Deshpande puts it, "The classics seem contemporaries of all ages. They have something to tell us in every context and in every situation in which we find ourselves. The great classics of our country have had an educative effect on the people of our land. When we are in distress, when we are in trouble, we turn to them, and they give us practical wisdom and spiritual comfort. They give us not merely enlightenment, they give us solace of mind also. The *Ramayana*, the *Mahabharat*, Kalidasa's works, in all of them these virtues are to be found. They give us examples as to how men should behave in different situations of life. Every day we must read a classic, not a mere textbook, not mere notes given by your teachers, which may serve you for your examinations, but turn your attention to some old classics of the East or West. All of them have the same power to stimulate your minds, to soothe your hearts; to enrich your whole nature, to make you a new being altogether."

Classics are not easy to digest at early stages of reading. These take longer time to read. Particularly, if it is from some other country or culture, it is all the more difficult to digest. Therefore, there are two easy methods of getting inducted to classics.

The first method is to refer to works such as *Masterpieces of World Literature,* by Frank N. Magill. It covers both fictions and nonfictions. It includes well-known novels, plays and poems and non-fiction - great works of philosophy and political theories.

This book covers 275 classics of the Western civilization. For each work covered, it gives a concise plot summary, descriptions of major characters, all the important facts of date and authorship and a critical evaluation.

Similarly, *Masterpieces of African-American Literature* is also available in the same series. These books are available in large libraries. *The Reader's Companion to World Literature* Edited by Lillian Herlands Hornstein, G. D. Percy, and Calvin S. Brown, *Books that Changed the World* by Robert Downs are some similar titles. *Sacred Books of the East* is another such 'masterpiece' series.

[If your nearest library does not have these titles, you suggest them to the librarian.] In short, if complete classic is not available, read at least such collected classics in digest form.

The second method is to access abridged editions of classics. Also look for Ulverscroft Large Print Books. Ulverscroft Foundation has brought out most of classics in large print. These books are easy to read not only for low-vision persons but also for normal readers. Such books sustain young readers' attention.

These publications are ideal for introducing youngsters and busy readers to classics.

Stage 3B: Introduction to Nonfiction : In case of fictions and plays it is the story that holds the attention of readers. This is difficult to achieve in case of nonfictions. But, this category does not mean textbooks or such academic learning materials.

Self-help books are very ideal to begin nonfiction or purposive reading. There are many popular titless by C.N.Parkinson and M.K Rustomji. These are serious self-improvement management books. Some of the titles by these authors are *Getting Along Better with People, 134 Tips for the Go-ahead Manager, Business is People, 109 Ways of Getting to the Top, Excellence in Management, Great Ideas in Management, The Paperwork Jungle, How to Enjoy Your Work and Succeed* etc.

The main feature of these books is their presentation. Each page has a caricature and some text, not exceeding 200 words related to the idea expressed. There is very little to read, but a lot to learn. This makes reading a pleasure.

There are many books in this class, such as One Minute Manager series, hobby books, spiritual books, collection of articles etc are good starting points for nonfictions.

Stage 3C: Language and Reading : Good ideas and good culture may come from any language. In this sense language and reading have no relationship. It should not matter which language, so long as there is good content. You may read in any language in which you have proficiency.

True, but language has some influence on reading. Generally, we find it easy to read in mother tongue. Reading is faster in mother tongue as comprehension is easy.

My personal view is that we should read mythology, spiritual content, yoga etc in our mother tongue. It is nice to learn an Indian subject in an Indian language. [Those who had pre-primary onwards all education in English language, may have to read everything in English.] But, for other professional subjects English is ideal, as major research output is reported in that language. In other words, if I have to read something about Chanakya or Buddha, I should read it in my mother tongue. If it is any management or professional literature, I should prefer English text.

Thus, a person should develop reading habits in fiction and nonfiction in both mother tongue and English. After 20 years of age a reader is free to read anything he wishes.

4.2. A TENTATIVE PLAN FOR READING

The previous section explained how reading habit has to be cultivated among children. [Technique is same even for adults. Even now, I love reading *Chandamama* or comics.] Well, can a student who is studying in school/college, handling homework, assignments, regular tests etc., facing examinations, shaping his educational career give so much time for general reading as it is expected in the previous section? In addition, the child also needs to play. Outdoor games are equally important in development of a child. Where do we get time to do all this? We need to draw up a plan.

Before drawing a plan, let us examine a feeling that extra reading -the kind of reading suggested in the previous section- is a hindrance for scholastic studies. How far is this idea true?

In order to encourage reading general books, in addition to textbooks among school children, the Ministry of Education, Government of India sponsored a Project entitled "Reading for Pleasure" in 1957. Seven schools in Delhi were selected and a total of 614 students - 435 boys and 179 girls - from these schools participated in the project. The duration of the project was six months only, from August 1957 - January 1958. The number of books read by these students was 5523 at the rate of nine books per student.

When the annual examinations were held, it was found that these students had fared better than the others who were content with studying only textbooks. The vocabulary of these 614 students was vaster, their power of expression was better, their general knowledge extensive, and they obtained more marks. This disproves the cold belief among laymen, that extra reading beyond textbooks affects the performance of the students at exams. Later a National Conference on Reading was held from 5 to 7 May 1958, and it recommended that schools should encourage general reading among students and libraries should be established in all schools. (India, Ministry of Education.1959. *Reading for Pleasure: Proceedings of the First National Conference on Reading.*)

But, not all students, teachers and parents know about this study and its findings. Nevertheless, general reading has to be accommodated within the framework of scholastic studies. I am presenting a plan based on responses of many readers of the British Council Library, Madras (Chennai).

- During the working days of school/college concentrate only on newspaper reading in addition to scholastic studies.
- Assign one hour a day for general reading other than news and scholastic material. In that, read feature articles in magazines, *Reader's Digest*, film reviews, book reviews etc.
- Read at least two small books in a month, such that extra reading does not cut into your scholastic reading. Devote at least one or two hours a day for outdoor playing.
- During the vacation, increase general reading. This is the time to read Akbar-Birbal, Tenali Ram to *Masterpieces of World Literature* to abridged works, biographies, plays etc. In Diwali and Christmas vacation you may give two hours a day for such general reading.

- It is essential for children to read titles from *Amar Chitra Katha* series. The series was introduced by Mr. Anant Pai in 1967 to teach Indian children about our cultural heritage. It is a series of comic books with over 400 titles in over 20 Indian languages and in English brought out by India Book House.
- The titles in this series cover stories of mythological characters and biographies of Indian personalities. *Tinkle* is another similar anthology for children.
- There is too much to read, and too little time. Learn to prioritise. Choose titles based on some criteria. Think of the purpose of reading. (Please see the next chapter.)
- During summer vacation you may spend more time - perhaps up to four hours- on general reading. Master some hobbies during vacation. It could be yoga, music, magic, origami etc. Also learn cycling, swimming etc. and read about these hobbies/skills.
- Watch movies and television programmes, both commercial and those based on classics.

This leads to all-round growth of a child.

After knowing what to read and when, the next essential component of reading habit, is to know why do we read.

5

Purpose and Materials for Reading

Although we strongly believe that there are no bad books, human history is punctuated with instances of banning and burning of books and the banishing of authors, proving again and again that the 'Pen is mightier than the Sword'. Perhaps what this paradox means is that books are not bad, their effect on humanity could be bad. The effect is not induced from outside (i.e. by the books) but is caused in the minds of the men who read.

Thus, there is a potential danger caused by some books. Rather, damage is not caused by books, but by the immaturity or ignorance or tender age of the reader. It could be due to political or religious affiliations. Nevertheless, there is need to exercise some restraint, though not censorship. The restraint may be exercised by authors or editors or librarians or the individuals who select the books from market.

Regarding such restraint, a blogger librarian had once said, "Everyone has the right to choose what to read. I don't intend to force my choice on to anyone. I can choose not to read a book with any objectionable sensitive text, if I don't want to. But nobody should be deprived of the opportunity to broaden their horizons in any which way they wish to. Such openness is good when the reader is an adult and is capable of making his choice. This absolute freedom can not be and should not be given to developing minds."

I echo these views. Therefore, selection of books and reading materials by parents, teachers, professionals, librarians and even by individuals is necessary. Selection is required as too many books are published, and it is not possible to purchase every book appearing in the market. Neither do we have that much of money nor space to keep those books.

This choosing or selecting a book is not merely for purchasing. Even if you have to borrow a book from a library, you can not read every thing available in a library. Choosing or prioritizing depends on purpose of reading.

5.1. PURPOSE OF READING

A major purpose for reading is considered to be learning. In order to know the purpose of reading, we must know the learning strategies of adults. It is often interpreted as the process of engaging adult learners with the structure of learning experience. This is covered under a concept called andragogy, a theory of adult education by the American educationist Malcolm Knowles.

Knowles' theory is based on six assumptions related to motivation of adult learning.

a. Adults need to know the reason for learning something.
b. Experience provides the basis for learning activities (Foundation).
c. Adults need to be responsible for their decisions on education; they want involvement in the planning and evaluation of their instruction.

d. Adults are most interested in learning subjects having immediate relevance to their work and/or personal lives.

e. Adult learning is problem-centered rather than content-oriented.

f. Adults respond better to internal versus external motivators.

In short, andragogy aims at self-directed education. In the same way, reading also should be self-directed, result-oriented and purpose-driven.

Broadly speaking, there are four purposes for reading.

- **To understand** or know or comprehend new concepts. The purpose in this sense is to internalize the information and understand the essence of what is read. To find out what a book is mostly about is the broad purpose.
- **To assess** or evaluate a subject. In this sense, it is knowing the pros and cons of a subject or concept to interpret or infer cause and effect of a phenomenon.
- **To apply** the gathered information or to find a specific topic in a book or article. A student reads a textbook to pass an examination, a lawyer reads to argue his case, a teacher reads to prepare his lecture. It is to learn some subject matter that is required for a scholastic purpose.
- **For recreation** or for pleasure. This includes light reading such as fictions, magazine articles etc. To be aimless is the aim in this type of reading. Most of recreational readings are for personal amusement or knowledge. There are no professional or educational reasons.

In short, why do we read a particular text? Is it for information or for knowledge or for application or for recreation? In other words, it could be for enjoyment, to present it to others, to answer questions, to get information.

The purposes of reading point at two different, but related issues.

- Depending on the purpose of reading, there are different methods available for reading. Effective and knowledgeable readers learn to use different styles and techniques of reading for different purposes. Skimming, scanning and critical reading are the three major styles of reading.
- There are different types of reading materials available for different purposes. Textbooks, journals, magazines, reference sources, newspapers, novels, manuals, mails, web pages etc meet different purposes of reading. These are just a few of the things that people read every day.

Now these issues are considered in details.

5.2. PURPOSE AND METHOD OF READING

Different methods of reading have been evolved for different purposes. Three major methods of reading have been identified for three major purposes. [The four purposes identified are built into these three main reasons.] Similarly, the three methods can be considered as combinations of some techniques. These techniques are discussed in the next chapter.

a. For General Information: Skimming

If you want to find general information about a subject, you have to skim through a book or many documents to determine how these are organized and what they cover. You have to flip through the pages quickly to get an overview. You can find out whether it has the required information. [See p. 69-70]

If you are reading a book or an article for recreation or you simply want to know about a specific topic, then you want to read fast. You need not read every word. You don't have to know the meaning of every word of the passage; you can guess it based on the context.

b. For Specific Information: Scanning

When you want to know the meaning of a word or specific bit of information, you need to scan a dictionary or a book or an article. When you scan you know what you are searching. You scan the title, the table of contents, the headings and the index to find out if the required information is available. [See p. 70]

c. For Learning: Systematic or Critical Reading

A reader wants first to skim a book or chapter to know what it covers. Then he will look at the headings and subheadings to find out how the book is organized. He should link between what he already knows and the reading material. This is purposive reading. [See p. 71-72]

Once the reader has a general idea about the material he wants to learn, he will read the sections carefully and slowly. He tries to understand every word with the help of a dictionary or a glossary. After reading the chapter or section carefully, he revises the material and tries to answer questions about the document.

[SQ4R, Skimming, Scanning, Systematic/Critical Reading including Light Reading and Word by Word Reading are covered as techniques in the next chapter. Here these are treated from the reading purpose angle.]

5.3. PURPOSE AND TYPES OF READING MATERIALS

Each purpose of reading is met by a specific type of reading material. Thus, purpose and the method of reading are interrelated. Here is an attempt to list a few types of documents and indicate the methods of reading those texts. (types of reading material and corresponding tips)

i. Reading Newspapers

Newspapers are arranged in sections. If you are familiar with a newspaper, you can directly go to the sections of your interest skipping the other sections altogether. We know sports section is at the end; similarly we know where editorials appear, when and where film reviews and book reviews appear etc. In case you are not familiar, browse through the publication for a few days. Soon you get to know how to locate what you want. Make a mental note of its layout.

Read newspaper articles by scanning down the column, digesting all the words across, instead of reading each word at a time. A newspaper column usually has 4 or 5 words per line. All the words in a line should be read at once and should move down to the next line.

Identify the articles of your interest. Reading for information should be a 'goal seeking' activity. You should read or skim through it depending on how much time you have.

Newspaper articles focus on the most interesting and glamorous aspects of a topic. Their interest lies in circulation figure and not providing full understanding of a subject

Articles within newspapers and magazines tend to be in three main categories:

News articles : Here, the most important information is presented in the first paragraph (Intro), and with less and less useful details as the article progresses. This is called 'Inverted Pyramid' style. [Reporters are trained to write in 'Inverted Pyramid' style. It helps editors to cut latter paragraphs in a hurry to accommodate more news stories.] You can get the key facts in intro paragraphs. Read further, only if you need more details.

Opinion Articles : Opinion articles or 'Editorials' present a point of view. Here, the most important information is in the introduction and the summary, with the middle of the article supporting arguments.

Feature Articles : These are features to provide entertainment or background on a subject. Most important information is in the body of the text.

If you can recognize the category of an article, you can extract information from it.

Review headlines and select articles based on your interest, read the first paragraph to preview the article. More than 80% of the key information is found in it. The subsequent supporting text should be read only as needed. Follow SQ4R technique. [See p. 66-68] Then move on to the next article. The process should not take more than 10-15 minutes.

When reading news from any source, skip what you already know. Look for the information to match your purpose for reading. Spend 15-20 minute in the morning to browse the newspaper. This hurry forces you to get focused. In the evening take a look at the newspaper to see what you wanted to read. You may find that you are no longer interested in it.

When you read the newspaper, you're probably not reading it word-by-word, instead you're scanning the text. In Arnold Bennett's *How to Live on 24 Hours a Day* (1910), he narrates how he used to read five newspapers -some French and the rest in English, every day. He explains, "Newspapers are made in hurry, and they have to be read in hurry."

ii. Reading Journals/Magazines

Scan the table of contents or indexes of the magazine issue and turn directly to the articles you are interested in. Be sure what you want from an article, and why do you need to know its content. This makes it easy to extract information from it quickly and efficiently.

Step 1: Get maximum information in a minute by simply reading the title, subtitle, bold type, last paragraph and first paragraph. Then think of the relevance of the content for you. If it is relevant to you, go to the next step. Otherwise, move on to some other article.

Step 2: Skim through the article and find the central idea. Move to the next step if you need more details. Else, begin with another article.

Step 3: Read and find what you need. Make your notes, write down the details of the reference or keep a photocopy, if you are likely to use it later.

File the photocopy in a folder, and build a collection of related articles for future use.

iii. Books

In case of reading books, there are several steps:

- Know who the author is and the date of publication. [This gives a mindset which helps in deciding whether to read it further or not, and if 'yes', this information is of use in actual reading.]
- Scan through the preface and table of contents.
- Take a look at the diagrams, charts, tables and pictures, if any.
- First, skim the first and last chapters. This may give you all the required information.
- Then, read the first and last chapters and skim the intervening chapters. [Consider reading the first sentence of each paragraph.]
- Refer a dictionary or the glossary or index if needed.
- Regarding reading a book, you need to distinguish between types of reading, and then fit your reading style to suit the needs of the material.

A special note is necessary about reading poetry and plays. These types of books have to be read a few times - aloud and silently alternately- to get the essence of them. It is only then that we can get complete sense of its imagery, rhyme, intonation and other craftsmanship associated with them. This method is prescribed by Prof. Earl Daniels in *The Art of Reading Poetry.*

iv. Technical Books [Science, Technology, Economics, Management etc.]

While reading technical books, there is no need to **skip any text. Each paragraph is to be read with understanding of the context.** Technical books require a variety of reading skills. Use the common reading skills along with familiarity to the following concepts.

In case of technical books, an understanding about grouping or classification, the process method which involves certain procedures in a sequence of steps and the concept of 'cause and effect' are necessary. Similarly, precise definitions, ideas of experimental methods etc. are essential.

Authors use many methods in their scientific discussions. Familiarity with these methods is necessary in understanding the ideas.

Reading an academic book requires concentration. It takes more time and effort. You may need to read a section a number of times and make your notes. If you find the topics difficult to understand, read a few elementary books on the subject. Read an encyclopaedic article. Try tutorials, PowerPoint presentations and images on the net.

v. Reference Books

These books are not meant for cover-to-cover reading. Such books are referred for some specific bit of information, hence these are called reference books. Dictionaries, encyclopedias, gazetteers, glossaries, atlases, directories, yearbooks, indexes, abstracts etc are the examples of such type. These books are arranged in alphabetical or chronological or some other specific order. The topics are disjointed, and hence not meant for continuous reading.

These books are ideal for scanning. These titles are supported by an exhaustive index to facilitate quick scanning and searching. In case of multi volume encyclopedias, one can access an article by scanning. After accessing, the article has to be read as any other article.

vi. Manuals

Manuals are often supplied with a product as an after-sales procedure and to improve handling of the product. It may be prepared by junior professionals or may not have been properly edited.

As a first step, find out if it is written for operator level or engineers' level. It should not be too basic, nor should it be too advanced. Make sure that you have the manual at the right level.

Use the table of contents and index to find the right section. It is necessary to skim before reading in details.

It is better to copy the glossary and machine drawings or schematic diagrams to facilitate quick reference. Write your own notes with a graphic explanation and mind map.

vii. Reports, Proposals etc

If you are reading a document, such as a proposal or a report, which presents an overall analysis of a subject, it is possible to accept the writer's structure of thought. In such event, we may not know that important aspect has been overlooked or some irrelevant detail has been covered.

Therefore, in case of such documents, it is better to have your own table of content or structure before you open the document. You can then use this structure to read the document in the order that you want.

With this technique you can spot what is missing and helps you to avoid less significant details. In case the writer has a better structure, it helps you to bridge the gaps in your knowledge and modify your views.

Once the purpose –even a combination of purposes- for reading is established, a reader can choose the reading material and decide which method of reading suits to achieve that purpose.

Each person reads different documents for different purposes at different times. A professional may read a newspaper in the morning for information, a learned journal for gaining a cutting edge in his work, read a fiction for amusement and a comic for his child.

A person may read William Shakespeare's plays for recreation when he is in early young age. As a researcher, the same person may read it word by word and try to understand the social history of that time or psychology of the characters etc.

Efficient readers learn to use different strategies for different kinds of reading. They know when it's fine to read quickly – skipping over some of the words, how to skim for general information, scan for specific information, and how to study for tests or for research. But, to become an expert reader, one must be familiar with these reading techniques. These techniques will be introduced in the following chapter.

6

READING TECHNIQUES

We have seen that as we grow, the pictorial part in books reduces giving way to the text component. Correspondingly, the method of reading also changes. But majority of people do not even know that there are different methods of reading.

In early years of our life, we learn to read alphabets then we combine alphabets in a word and read those words. Then gradually we move on to read sentences with two, three, four and more words. By this time, we learn to understand syntax (order of words in a sentence) and other grammatical nuances. For example, we learn to distinguish the meanings of the following sentences.

- He gave me one hundred rupees only. [Nothing more, nothing less]
- He gave me only one hundred rupees. [This has two meanings. Nothing other than that and he did not give it to others]
- He only gave me one hundred rupees. [I did not ask, He only....]
- Only he gave me one hundred rupees. [Nobody else gave me.]

Thus, we learn how writing, reading, intonation and meaning/comprehension are related. We also realise that comprehension is more important than mere reading. Reading process includes the following steps.

- See and identify the alphabets and words.
- Then we learn to read word by word, one word at a time.
- Identify a combination of words in a specific order as a sentence.
- Understand the message -with meaning and feeling-conveyed through a group of sentences.

Some people think that it is only the last step which is considered reading. But it can not happen without the first three; these are presumed. Others consider the first three steps as reading and presume that the fourth automatically happens. Both have some justifications. Neither should take backseat. Here lies the essence of different reading methods/techniques. We learn these techniques as we grow.

6.1. NORMAL READING TECHNIQUES

Reading as we have seen in the previous section is suitable up to school level. There is more to read and less time is available. Not every document need to be read cover to cover. Hence, different techniques are adopted.

A. SQ4R

SQ4R is a popular technique of reading and studying. It is a technique evolved and approved by educational psychologists. SQ4R is an abbreviation that stands for Survey, Question, Read, Recite, Relate, Review. These can be considered as steps of reading or studying. Let us examine each of these components or steps.

a. Survey : Before we start reading, it is necessary to survey the book and the chapter or an article that is to be studied. In case of books, go through the blurb, contents page, introduction, appendix etc. At a chapter or an article level, a survey means a quick glance at the title, headings and subheadings.

In addition, see the pictures, charts, graphs, maps etc, if any, along with captions. Just read introductory and concluding paragraphs. Also see what chapters come before and after the current one. Also, read the summary or abstract if the document is a journal article.

b. Question : During the process of surveying, a few questions emerge in your mind. These questions are triggered by the genuine curiosity. A question may stem from the title or a heading or anything that is seen while surveying. Also ask yourself, what you already know about the subject, and what you intend to know. In other words, a structure is framed in the mind. The process of reading should fill in the structure.

Also, question the author's ideas and their authenticity. Questioning actively involves you in the learning process. Read to search.

Formulation of questions is facilitated by Rudyard Kipling's famous lines.

I keep six honest serving men

They taught me all I knew

Their names are What and Why and When

And How and Where and Who.

c. Read : Now start reading. While you are reading, find the answers to the questions raised in the previous step. Understanding the questions and trying to find answer helps you in reading actively. Reading without questions may become a passive exercise. Questions keep you oriented and attentive.

Read one section at a time and recite after each section. Read slowly the portions difficult to comprehend. Consider rereading the parts that are not clear.

d. Recite : Silently summarize what you have read, in your own words. Reciting may be done after each paragraph or each section or chapter, depending on your requirement and the complexity of the text. Prepare notes in your own words. Focus on the answers as you read, recite and prepare notes. Underline or highlight important points. Identify the key issues.

e. Relate : Relate the new information gathered to what is already known to you. Draw parallel to something closer to you or your observation or experience. Try to remember by association.

f. Review : After reading, take an overview of the chapter or the article, as it was done while surveying. Test your own memory by reciting. In this process the newly read content is internalized, and it becomes part of your knowledge. You may need to review frequently.

Review should include other related material such as glossaries, self-tests etc. Frequent reviewing will substantially reduce the time you need to preparing for exams, and the process will be less stressful.

[Regarding the 4Rs in this methods, there are different versions presented in different sources. While some use 'Read, Recite, Record, Review', others have preferred 'Read, Reflect, Recite, Review '. Here I have considered 'Read, Recite, Relate, Review'. 'Record' is considered part of 'Recite'. 'Relate' includes 'Reflect'.]

SQ4R is an ideal way of reading to study any subject. It has capacity to zoom-out and zoom-into any subject/ text.

[Source: http://www.wvup.edu/academics/learning_center/sq4r_reading_method.htm
http://ababasoft.com/speedreading/r043.html]

B. Skimming

Skimming is a process of visually searching the text to quickly identify the main ideas. It is letting your eyes catch keywords. This can give you a rough idea of the meaning of the material. Although it is a natural way of searching information, some persons find it difficult. Usually this skill may not be acquired by practice; it is considered a gift. Some consider it as skill and others consider it as a gift. Skimming is mostly employed by adults and not much by kids.

There are three types of skim reading processes.

- Consider reading the first sentence of each paragraph. This technique is useful when you are seeking specific information rather than reading for comprehension. Often the first sentence of each paragraph gives the central idea, and the other sentences elaborate on that idea. Therefore, you can get enough information by only reading the first sentence from each paragraph.
- Some people read the first and last paragraphs and using headings, summaries and other organizers used by the author as you move down the page or screen. You might read the title, subtitles, subheadings and illustrations.
- Another form of skimming is that commonly employed by readers on the Web. This involves skipping over text that is less interesting or relevant.

Our normal reading speed is around 200 words per minutes (wpm). With skimming the speed increases to over 400 to 500 wpm or more.

Here you read quickly to know whether the text is of use to you or not. You are not searching for a specific item and keyword. Skimming provides an 'overview' of the text. It is useful to look at chapter/section headings, summaries and opening paragraphs. The purposes of skimming are:

- To check relevance of the text.
- To set the scene for more concentrated effort to follow, if the text is found useful.

Skimming should be used only for general purpose reading. It works well to find dates, names, and places. It might be used to review graphs, tables and charts. It is useful when you have a lot to read.

Skimming should not be done for serious reading. In case of information-intensive reading material, skimming reduces comprehension. It is used for light reading.

C. Scanning

Scanning is a technique to be employed when you are looking up for a specific word in a document. Scanning is a process of moving your eyes quickly down the text, searching specific words, phrases or ideas. In such cases, you know what you are searching for. Therefore, you are concentrating only on finding a particular bit of information.

In scanning,

- You are looking for specific information, quickly.
- You know what you are searching for.
- You 'see' every item on the page, but you don't necessarily read the pages - you ignore anything you are not interested in.

When scanning, keep observing the author's method of organization of ideas. Notice how he/she has used numbers, letters, steps etc. to separate the ideas/concepts/words. Notice the order of concepts, alphabetical, numerical or spatial etc. Look for words that are bold faced, italics, or in a different font size, style, or colour. Sometimes the author will put key ideas in the margin. All these techniques help in scanning process.

Scanning is the technique used while searching a telephone book or dictionary or an index.

D. Purposive Reading

Purposive Reading is a combinational of the above stated methods. The stated categories are not mutually exclusive. There are times when we need a blend of SQ4R, skimming and scanning. Here a part of the document needs quick scanning, then understand the various issues involved and study a section of it in depth. Here the reader chooses a method depending on his purpose at that moment. It is a sort of critical reading.

Reading from a computer screen has become a growing concern. Research shows that people have more difficulty reading from a computer screen than from paper. Although they can read and comprehend at the same rate as on paper, skimming on the computer is much slower than on paper.

Well, purposive reading can be of two types.

a. Light Reading : Here reading is for pleasure and tends to be 'light' in nature. It could be a leisure activity. This form of reading does not generally require detailed study and concentration. The text has to be read at a pace comfortable to the reader. There are no fixed techniques. However, one may consider the following points.

- Read with understanding.
- Understand the feelings and sentiments of the author and the characters in the book.
- Skim the boring, irrelevant passages.

b. Word by Word Reading : This type of reading is time consuming and demands a high level of concentration. Some material is not readily understood and so requires a slow and careful analytical reading. People use this type of reading for unfamiliar subjects, scientific formulae etc.

Source: http://ababasoft.com/speedreading/five_types_of_reading.htm

In addition, there are a few other types of reading as part of Critical Reading. These are,

- **Audible Reading** is for reading and appreciating poetry and drama.
- **Close Reading** for mastering and internalizing information.
- **Exploratory Reading** is for exploring or gaining acquaintance with information.
- **Review Reading** is for refreshing or brushing up the memory. This is to revise something which is already known, but temporarily out of touch. Or reading something which is already read. One tends to read the portions which the reader had enjoyed earlier.

These techniques are considered as normal, because one acquires these skills by some minimal efforts to learn them. These skills are acquired by natural instinct/ intuition.

It is a heuristic (trial and error) method. If you are lucky, you may get a good mentor or a guru at the right time in life to tell about such skills. These reading skills, purposes and documents are given on the next page in a tabular form.

An average reading speed of a common man is in the range of 150 to 200 wpm. Skimming and scanning may increase speed up to 500 or 700 wpm; but it can be applied only to certain types of documents.. It is required to increase reading speed proportionally for all other types of documents also. The need for such speed reading is indicated in the next section.

6.2. SPEED READING

Reading speed has to be increased because there is an information overload. There is so much to read, and so little time available.

Reading Techniques and Purposes at a Glance

Reading Technique	Purpose of Reading	Documents
SQ4R	To study, familiarise, understand and update	Research Papers, Articles, Textbooks
Skimming	To know the main ideas	Newspapers
Scanning	Searching	Dictionaries, Telephone Directories, Indexes, Web pages,
Purposive Reading or Critical Reading with SQ4R	To identify, understand and apply	Reports, Proposals, Manuals, Standards, Specifications, E-mails, Minutes of Meetings, Correspondence etc.
Light Reading	Recreation/Enjoyment	Fictions, Poetry, Satires, Essays
Word by Word Reading	Literature Review, Research	Any of the documents from the above lists so long as the purpose of reading is research

Reading speed is critical to our professional success. Professionals have to read business letters, reports, proposals, books, manuals, journal articles, trade literature etc. If they do not read all these, at the right time, they are found lagging behind in their professional circle and among their colleagues. Therefore, your reading speed is crucial to your performance and income earning potential.

In these days of multi-tasking, getting spare time for reading is very difficult.

Hence, it is necessary to acquire speed reading techniques. Speed reading is not one single technique. It is a set of techniques.

In intial years of education, we learn to read one word at a time and that too loudly. This vocalizing the words takes a lot of time. From here we need to step up our reading speed. Here is an attempt to give a few general procedures and a few special techniques of fast reading.

[This is just an indicative outline and not an exhaustive coverage. Readers are suggested to read books on speed reading or go through websites and web based tutorials.]

a. Initial/ General Techniques

As we grow, we start reading silently. This increases the speed, but we are still uttering or saying the words that we read silently in our mind. This is called subvocalizing. This gives the reader a comfortable feeling that he is reading, concentrating and understanding. [We cover this aspect a little later; it is one of the steps to increase reading speed.]

Observe your reading process. You see one word at a time and your eyes take some time to move from one word to the next. This has to be tackled first. The method used is called metaguiding.

b. Metaguiding

Metaguiding is a type of helping the eyes to move forward using a finger or a pencil or any other pointer. The pointer is made to move along the text by the reader. This helps the eyes to move faster along the lines of the text.

The pointer moves along a line and then moves to the next line taking the gaze along with it. The pointer should move along any of shapes shown in the figure.

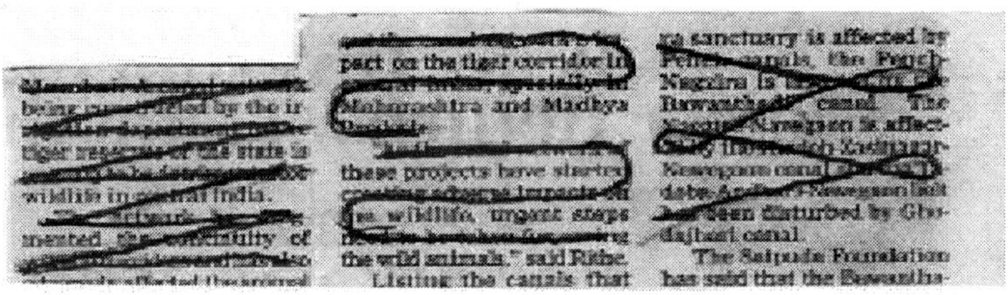

It helps in order to broaden the visual span for speed reading. **Instead of seeing one word at a time, eyes get trained to see three or four or more words at a time. Further, this exercise helps in increasing your** visual span to take in the whole line at a time. **It facilitates your eye to skim over the text, but the process may reduce comprehension and memory. Some important details of the text may escape the attention of the reader. Make sure each word in the sentence has been seen as you skim; you do not want to miss important words such as "not" and "maybe".**

c. Subvocalisation

Subvocalization is vocalising or pronouncing each word in mind as one reads. It is the internal speech made allowing the reader to imagine the sound of the word as it is read. This is a natural process. Readers subvocalizes such that they make visible movements on the lips, jaw, or throat. Although some of these visual signs may disappear as one practises, subvocalization remains with a reader. **While**

reading a text, it helps the mind to reduce its pressure and grasp meaning. Subvocalisation enables to comprehend and remember what is read.

It is felt that subvocalization "places extra burden on the cognitive resources, thus, slowing the reading down." The problem is that this habit means that you can only read as fast as you can talk, which is about 200 wpm. [Source: http://ababasoft.com/subvocalization/spesial_rhythm.html]

Subvocalization is an old habit that dies hard.

Some methods are suggested to convince how subvocalization affects speed and comprehension.

Try to read a text in your mind (of course with subvocalization) and at the same time start counting loudly. Or you should make some conscious hand movements in a rhythm as you read. We realize how difficult it is to do both. This suggests that reading and subvocalisation can not be done simultaneously. When we get rid of subvocalisation, reading speed and comprehension improves.

d. Upper Gaze

Upper gaze is reading by moving your eyes along the upper half of a line of the text. This technique is based on the belief that it takes more time to read if the reader has to see the entire word and the line. Human mind is capable to read and comprehend without the lower half of the line. The upper gaze of the line helps to move the eyes fast over the line. [If you try with lower half of the line does not give such result.

a. Lower Gaze (Difficult to Read)

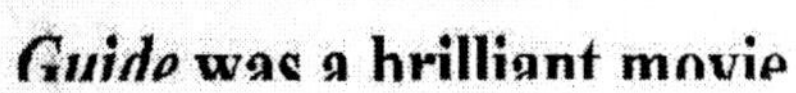
b. Upper Gaze (Easy to Read)

e. Skipping

Skipping certain words in the text and moving forward your gaze results in achieving more speed. Cloze Test or C-test, as more popularly known, is primarily used for teaching fast reading and also in measuring readability. It is based on Gestalt theory that mind can supply the missing words in a text. Thus, certain words in the text become redundant and the time spent in reading those missing words is saved. In C-test, sentences are presented with say, every fifth or seventh word is replaced by three dots.

Example: *"Anyone who falls from such a ... can not ...."*

I am sure you can read this sentence with the two words missing. It is now easy for you to get convinced that you can skip certain routine words and increase reading speed.

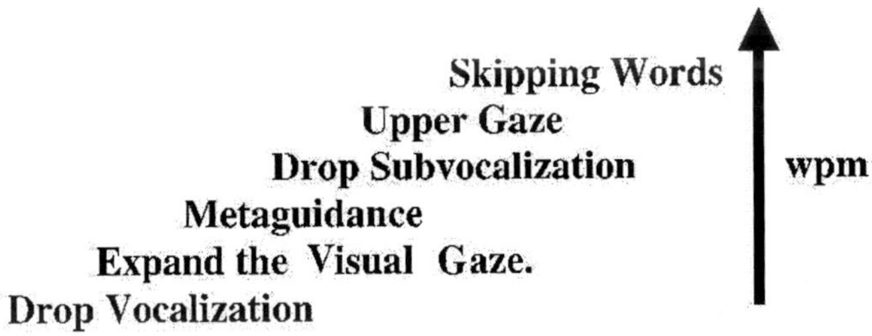

The speed reading techniques are shown diagrammatically in the above figure.

Different techniques of reading outlined in this chapter will surely help initiate a beginner to improve his/her reading speed.

But, as in case of any other skill, it needs proper training and practice. You can not learn swimming or horse riding by reading a book on these skills. It requires training and practice.

Increasing the speed is one side of the coin. The other side is comprehension. By mastering the skills outlined here one can acquire up to 2000 wpm. But, what is the use, if we can not comprehend it, if we can not recall when required? This issue calls for detailed discussion.

7

READING AND COMPREHENSION

Comprehension in relation to reading, is the understanding of what is written in the document. If a book or any other text is read by two individuals, both will not have the same understanding of the document. Thus, different individuals have different levels of comprehension of the same document, leave alone of different reading materials. Why does it happen like that?

7.1. FACTORS OF COMPREHENSION

When we read a passage we connect or relate the ideas on the page to what we already know. If we do not know anything about the subject, ther. we store the newly learned ideas into our mind. Both these processes - relating to the known ideas and acquiring new concepts- amount to comprehension.

Comprehension is dependent on motivation, mental structures for holding assorted ideas, concentration and study techniques.

- **Motivation and interest** are essential for every activity. If the reader is well motivated then he is mentally prepared and curious to take in any new idea. In addition, before actual reading if skimming is done, it generates curiosity. Similarly discussion with friends also generates desire to read. Skimming serves as an appetizer before a good dinner. It holds reader's interest and facilitates comprehension.

- **Broad Knowledge Base** of a reader helps in readily comprehending a new idea. Wide reading and wide travel help in this process. A person with better background has better comprehension.

- **Mental Structure** of the reader, and how far he/she is aware of it, is an important factor in comprehension. Just as there are pigeonholes to sort letters in post offices, our mind also has a structure based on our training and upbringing.

The imaginary pigeonholes can be created or modified consciously. It is like this; when I first time read **Rudyard Kipling's four lines [See p. 67], I created six pigeonholes in my mind. These are mentally labeled as** 'What', 'Why', 'How', 'Who', 'Where' and 'When'. I keep sorting the ideas I get while reading or listening into these slots. This helps me to identify definitions, causes/purposes, processes etc., even if an author has not written clearly.

Thus, the ideas in any writing have to be sorted into the reader's mind structure.

Well written documents have proper beginning, middle and end. Good writers present their ideas such that the first sentence of each paragraph gives an overview to help reader to sort the ideas into his mental structure. The rest of the sentences in the paragraph support or justify the idea.

- **Transitional words**, phrases or paragraphs provide link between the ideas. [Transitional expressions are, 'therefore', 'hence', 'in spite of' 'on the other hand'...etc.] A good writer has a large collection of such transitional expressions. The reader should note these expressions to comprehend the text.
- **Note the logic** used by the author. Is the narration straight cause and effect [It is ideal for social writings.] form or effect and cause [This is suitable for crime thrillers.] Notice whether author is following deductive logic [General to Specific] or inductive logic [Specific to General]. It is like top-down and bottom-up planning in presenting the ideas. Find the author's hypothesis, reasoning etc.
- **Anticipate** what may follow in the text while reading. If you are right, you will be happy, and if you are wrong, you will learn something new.
- **Graphics**, if any, help in comprehension. Even if the author has not provided any graphics, a reader can construct mental pictures to understand and remember the ideas.
- **Summarize** and review to develop a deeper understanding. Try to follow SQ4R [See p 66-68] to identify main points.

Good **vocabulary** and **concentration** are the two most essential prerequisites of better comprehension.

Any discussion about comprehension is incomplete without mention of two important issues. These are,

- Should we vocalize or subvocalize words for better comprehension?
- Is comprehension affected by speed reading?

7.2. SUBVOCALIZATION AND COMPREHENSION

Expert opinion about this issue is divided. Majority of the documents about speed reading believe that these two issues are inversely related. In other words, as subvocalization is reduced, speed increases and comprehension also increases.

However, there are some authors who feel that subvocalization, no doubt reduces speed, but it increases comprehension. This may be true up to an extent. But, your eyes must be trained to move forward while reading. Otherwise, when speed is reduced to increase comprehension, you may become so slow, that you forget a part of what is already read. Therefore, frequent backtracking becomes necessary, and it may further affect the speed of reading.

In conclusion, one need not get into the habit of subvocalization to increase comprehension.

7.3. SPEED AND COMPREHENSION

Generally people tend to think that comprehension declines as speed of reading increases. They are told right from their childhood to read slowly, understanding and remembering every word in the passage. This is an unfounded idea.

If you read slowly your mind may wander while reading. Once your concentration is lost, you may be mechanically reading but your mind is stuck elsewhere, and it is not registering any new idea. When your thoughts come back to the reading scenario, you may have lost link. Now you need to backtrack or regress and reread. This further slows down the reading process. Therefore, in reality slow reading does not increase comprehension.

On the other hand, consider you are reading a text fast. In that event you do not get time in between to think of anything else. The information received in the reading process is directly integrated into your memory structure. It forms a body of knowledge in your own words. You will remember it for longer duration, relate it to real life situations, develop applications, more readily than those things you remember verbatim. This really is comprehension.

In short, speed reading does not let the mind wander, and increases concentration and thus increases comprehension. But, how fast can one read?

In addition to the techniques covered in the previous chapter, there are highly powerful skills such as **Photo Reading** where our brain absorbs information directly from the page.

Photo Reading teaches you to look at a book differently. This is one of the secrets to **enable your whole mind to absorb information** as you flip through your reading material. It is claimed that with this skill one can read one page per second, which is about 25,000 words a minute. This technique is beyond the scope of this book and everyone does not need such a skill. But, let me convince you, how it is possible to read 25,000 wpm.

- Consider we can see and read five words of a line in a newspaper column at a time. [At this stage vocalization and subvocalization are possible.]
- You must have heard about a concept called 'persistence of vision'. It is a phenomenon related to the eye by which an image is thought to persist for approximately $1/25^{th}$ of a second on the retina even after it has disappeared. [This is the concept behind the working of cinema.]
- Thus, our sight can distinguish up to 25 pictures presented to our eyes. [Certain books give this as 20 images and some put it as 16 images per second.]

- Then, we can safely consider it as 5 × 25 = 125 words per second [After subvocalization is dropped.]
- Thus, in a minute one can read 125 × 60 = 7500 wpm.
- By using speed reading techniques, such as 'Upper Gaze' and 'Skipping Words' one can cross three times this speed. At such speed no other thought can pass through the reader's mind to distract him/her leading to better comprehension.

This is not easy to achieve. It requires practice under an expert trainer. Remember, the purpose of this book is to say that this is possible.

Reading is not a gymnastic exercise. It should be enjoyed consciously otherwise we may throw the baby with the bathwater. A normal adult can read 150 - 200 wpm. If he can achieve up to a maximum of 1000 wpm, it is satisfactory.

In addition, reading is not a vehicle with a single gear. We should know how to change gear depending on the road. Similarly, different types of literature need different speeds depending on how it is related to us.

The seven chapters in this part focused on developing and sustaining reading habit at an individual level. Parents and teachers can provide guidance at this stage. Even a reader can get self-help.

The next part deals with what book-trade, education system, public libraries and the Government should do to develop and sustain reading habit.

Part B :

Sustaining Reading Habit

8

Book Trade, Education System and Reading

Reading habit should not be something that we acquire in childhood or at some stage of life, and subsequently lose as we get busy with something else. You may be having that inner drive to read against all other pressures and constraints. You may even have acquired time management skills to accommodate reading component in your busy schedule. These are intrinsic factors. But, access to an uninterrupted supply of good books and reading materials depends on healthy book trade, which includes publishing and bookselling.

8.1. PUBLISHING

Publishing is the process of production and dissemination of printed or electronic information for the public or limited access. Publishing is an industry because big money is at stake. It includes selection of manuscripts and/or commissioning the authors to write on marketable themes, refereeing, copyediting, printing and other marketing related issues. The product of the publishing industry could be books, newspapers journals, magazines, musical works and other works providing information and software. This covers conventional and electronic versions.

There are many legal issues related to publishing such as copyright, defamation, partnerships, author-publisher agreements etc. Also, there are managerial issues like pricing, distribution etc.

Publishing, in relation to development and sustenance of reading habit, must deal with three aspects.

a. Choice of Themes is the essence of marketing. Certain publishers are known for certain subjects. Thus, the choice of theme is not really a macro problem. An exhaustive list of publishers by subject is available at, the following site. *http://www.publishersglobal.com/directory/list-publishing-subjects.asp*. But, there are micro issues. Publishers must select rare, innovative, socially relevant themes within their specialized domains. The selection should not be governed only by commercial reasons.

The level and graphic content should go hand in hand. A book about airplane can be written for aeronautical engineers or for children. The difference is in the level, language and graphics. The purpose of stressing this point is to tell that when a publisher chooses a manuscript for publishing, it is not only choice of subject, but also, the language, illustration and the level at which it has to be pitched based on the target readers etc. Each publisher selects manuscripts for publishing based on his understanding of what a reader would like to read.

There are many types of books available in the market. Types of books considering only the children's interest include the following.

- Wordless Picture Books
- Pattern Books
- Participation Books

- Language Play Books
- Alphabet Books
- Picture Dictionaries
- 3-D Books
- Talking Books (for blind persons and kids.)
- Comics
- Abridged editions of Classics etc.
- Ulverscroft Foundation's Large print editions

This is just a select list. For adults there are different forms such as poetry, drama, fiction, letters, essays, satire, published film scripts, biographies, autobiographies, travelogues, contemporary issues, adventure, reference sources etc.

Then, there are subject related books. Sometimes, publishers bring out combinations. An ideal example of such combination is Ken Blanchard's *One Minute Manager* Series. Titles in this series give complex management ideas in the form of conversation between fictitious characters. All these are the options available to the publishers.

b. Publicity of books is just bringing information about the existence of relevant titles to the potential readers. Besides conventional advertisements and book reviews, there are many ways of publicity. Having distribution channels, sending books for approval to libraries, organizing book exhibitions, book fairs are some of the techniques employed.

Internet has given a big boost to book trade. The success story of Amezon.com stemmed from book trade. Table of Content (TOC), book reviews, readers' views, sample chapters etc give excellent publicity. Any extra information about author, the theme, related prizes, awards etc. are hyperlinked, and hence these allied details are just a click away. A reader can directly buy a book using his credit card.

c. **Pricing** is a very critical aspect of the marketing mix. Price of a book is decided not only by the nature of book but also on the estimated sales of the title. When price is on the higher side, the books can be purchased only by libraries and institutions. Purchase at individuals' level and as gift item depends on the utility of a book and its price. Impulsive buying of books is possible when the price is within affordable limit.

Is reading habit related to price of book? You may have a temptation to think that these are related. No. these are not.

- In early 1990s Prof K. S. Deshpande gave an impressive lecture on 'Reading Culture' at the Karnataka Sangh, Mumbai. During the discussion, a young man grumbled, "Sir, books are very expensive. Each book costs over an average of 300 to 500 rupees. We can not afford to buy and read."

  Prof Deshpande responded in the form of another question. He asked, "Young man, what is the price of the pair of jeans and shoes you are wearing? You do not grumble for that. Buy at least 3-4 books every year and share them among friends. Let your friends also do the same thing. Thus, you will get a variety of reading material, and you do not feel the burden."
- With every passing year, cigarette and liquor are becoming more and more expensive. But, nobody has given up these habits because of the hike in the price.
- Even if all the published titles are given freely, do you think people will develop reading habits because books are free?
- Those who want to read will continue to read, no matter what the price is. They form a club, join a library or buy secondhand books, but somehow they keep reading. Those who would not like to read, keep on

discovering new excuses. Thus, reading habit is not related to the price of books.

This is equally applicable to the reading materials such as magazines and learned journals etc.

In spite of brave efforts of publishers, universities, 'National Book Trust, India', 'Children's Book Trust', RRRLF, Sahitya Akademi, etc., there is still a dearth of books both for children and the adults in India. Situation in the other developing countries is not much different.

The situation can be vastly galvanized by creation of a joyful atmosphere for authors to practise their creative craft. There should be schemes of awards and rewards to the authors. Book trade should be granted recognition as a major industry. The Government should allot vantage spots for bookshops and full blooded library network should be established in the country.

8.2. BOOKSELLING

Selling grocery, stationery, clothes, gold ornaments etc., are all meant for the physical body. These businesses are more profitable than selling books which embellish the mind and keep us humans. Result: there is a dearth of bookshops in the country. Even university towns do not have good bookshops. Network of bookshops like the Crossword, Landmark, Wheeler etc in metropolitan cities can be counted on fingers. Governments, city and town planners should allot centrally located attractive sites exclusively for bookshops.

It is a great feeling to find at least one bookshop in the malls. Most of the networked bookshops are interconnected. If you ask for a title, they not only check their stock, but also in the entire network. In case the title is not in the shop, but it is available in the branches, they offer to procure the title from wherever it is. If you wish to go to the branch where it is available, they even offer to set aside the title for you. They even offer to send the title through a courier to any place of your choice.

Whenever we talk about reading habit and book trade, we can not forget the role played by the secondhand bookshops on the pavements in developing and sustaining our reading habit. There are excellent bookshops on the pavements in Fort area and King Circle, Matunga in Mumbai. Such bookshops are in almost all the major cities and district headquarters.

Such secondhand bookshop owners' knowledge about books is amazing. They have good human network which enables them to supporting each others by directing the customers to the right bookshops or procuring from wherever it is.

Only one negative aspect of these pavement bookshops, at times, is the presence of pirated editions. Well, that is a shady area. We should be civilized enough to refuse to buy pirated books.

There are similar unconventional venues which help in sustaining reading habit. These are waiting rooms of clinics, beauty paralours and hair-cutting saloons, reception desks of corporate offices etc. All these provide light reading material while we are waiting to be attended.

I remember how frequently I used to go to a hair-cutting saloon to read *Illustrated Weekly, Eve's Weekly, Femina, Filmfare and Screen* etc. I cultivated warm friendship with the barber to access these reading materials. Similarly, the lobbies of corporate houses are good for browsing **coffee table books.**

8.3. EDUCATION SYSTEM

Our Education Policy and practice should aim at making some path-breaking decisions. Teachers should make students curious about the Nature and society than merely passing on information. Students should be made to reflect and internalize what they are learning. Emphasis should be laid on self-help to students.

Children at school should be taken to show bookshops, libraries, museums, zoos, parks, newspaper offices and television centres depending on their age and grasping level. [I remember we were taken to post-office, railway and radio stations by our school teachers.]

Whenever there is a book-fair, flower and fruits exhibition etc. students should be taken out to those places. These field observations should be supplemented by showing them additional information about all these in books. They should be made to connect what they see in Nature and society to what they get in books.

Invited speeches should be organized by authors, journalists and other media personalities. This serves as a great motivator in developing reading habit. The school projects should be so framed that it necessitates reading from libraries.

The implementation of these goals is possible, only if both teachers and students learn to read beyond the textbooks and cultivate the habit of reading for pleasure. Education should not be examination-centred. The aim of education must be to create a 'Society of Eternal Learners'. Without an abundant supply of books, how can these changes be brought in?

The current practice generally followed by teachers is to depend solely on the textbooks. Textbooks normally provide a uniform and good summary of the art/science. These are essentially adjusted and written to meet the level of the ordinary students, not the precocious or gifted ones.

Another shortcoming of the textbook is that it is conceived with an element of compulsion, which blocks full exploitation of the subject and never go beyond its immediate goal being an annual examinations. Therefore, textbooks are myopic in their content and treatment. You may get information, you may get through an examination, but you may not gain knowledge. You will not gain insight which is result of wide and supplementary reading.

A textbook has, therefore, been compared to a vitamin tablet, with which average students would be content. Not so the bright ones who would prefer 'a balanced nutritious wholesome meal'.

The late lamented justice Shri.M.C.Chagla, gratefully remembers his school teacher who led him from the severely limited textbooks into the vast unlimited world of other books. In his autobiography *Roses in December* (P.11 - 1974) he states thus:

"There was a teacher in the Dadar School who took special liking to me and who helped foster in me an interest in reading outside the textbooks prescribed for class room study. I owe an infinite debt of gratitude to him because my love of reading began from the time when this teacher opened to my eyes the long unending vistas of beauty and wisdom that lie within the covers of books written by the great authors of the past. But mainly it was to literature that he pointed his finger as a source which, if cultivated, would give me unbounded pleasure for the whole of my life."

It is important to get a knowledgeable mentor at the right age. In addition, you should have access to a good collection of books. It is also a fact that a majority of our schools are without good libraries; what they may be having are mere apologies for libraries. A good, generous, well organized, inviting library has to be an essential part of schools, if the aims of the new policy are to be entirely realized.

The combination of three issues, viz., reading beyond textbooks, escalating prices books and developing reading habit is complex in nature. It would be a good idea if the schools, colleges and other institutions decide to give books as gift to winners in various competitions.

Similarly, parents, friends and relatives must give books as gifts for occasions like birthdays and anniversaries etc. Even mementoes in various programmes should be in the form of books. It would be a modest step towards promoting reading habit.

9

LIBRARIES, LIBRARIANS AND READING

Library is an inseparable aspect of education and culture. Libraries play a great and significant role in developing and sustaining reading habits. However well motivated a reader may be, if his requirements are not met on day-to-day basis he may lose interest in reading.

No individual can buy all the books he likes to read; neither has he that much of money to buy nor space to store nor time to read. Libraries provide a variety of reading material without taxing you too much in terms of money and space. Role of libraries and librarians in developing and sustaining reading habits can be seen in the following paragraphs.

9.1. ROLE OF LIBRARIES IN EDUCATION

Each book in a library tries to tell something to its reader. It tries to teach him some lessons about social life and the Nature. Thus, every book and/or its author becomes a teacher. While a teacher in a classroom teaches a number of students at a time, a book or an author instructs a 'reader' on one-to-one basis, allowing each student to understand at any pace convenient to him or her. A collection of books therefore, automatically gets metamorphosed into a 'congregation of teachers'. Hence, Thomas Carlyle (1795-1881) the Scottish historian, declared, "A true university of the present day is a collection of books."

Libraries act as 'Resource Centers' for intellectual exercises. Libraries are actually 'consulting rooms'. Naturally therefore, libraries have to be managed by 'Professors of Books' - people who know books, love books, read and write books, and who would enjoy talking about books meaningfully.

Librarians and teachers constitute two sides of the same coin. Their roles are complementary to each other. The moment the teacher's job comes to a conclusion in the classroom, the librarian's task begins.

Teachers edify students with the help of textbooks, within a confined curriculum. The librarian, on the other hand, leads the students from a few into many other books, which supplement and augment knowledge contained in textbooks and class notes. Librarian cajoles them into wandering in the wonderful world of books. He/She talks with verve and enthusiasm about other interesting books related to their studies and also other books of abiding value.

A librarian has to be a scholar and a scientist first and then a skillful technician! He has to deliver a series of lectures, under 'User-Instruction' or 'User Education' or 'Orientation Programme'. In these sessions a librarian has to talk about the following issues.

- How the library is organized
- The role of books as "Teachers of Teachers"
- How to go about the job of making effective use of the book and periodical collection
- How information available in some other library can

be obtained on document delivery service and interlibrary loans

- How to use the internet for study purposes
- How to take down notes
- How to give citations etc.
- How to be in touch with new books [Book reviews, Amazon.com etc.]
- How to know the books of everlasting value

In educational institutions, this type of orientation programme is done once at the beginning of every academic year. May be it is done collectively or separately for each class of newcomers. But, in public and special libraries this exercise should be done whenever a new person joins the institution. The purpose is to make readers comfortable and 'feel at home' in the library. Orientation has a great role in developing reading habit among readers.

No matter whether it is an academic or public library, librarian has to form book clubs, organize book discussions, arrange topical and new books displays etc.

In essence, he has to act as a friend, philosopher and guide to the user, bearing in mind that the aim of education is not merely the bagging of degrees, or winning of gold medals, nor is it the securing of a good job. To achieve such a noble cause, the librarian has to be a person of great potential.

Almost the best person on the campus of an educational institution is the head of the institute, for example, the Vice-Chancellor of a University or the Principal of a College. But the next best man should be the Head of the Library. [This analogy holds true of other units like the District, City etc. town and village libraries.] It can be noticed in the well-known directories such as *World of Learning* and *Commonwealth Universities Yearbook* etc., that tne librarian's name is provided immediately after the vice-chancellor's name.

A librarian has to don the mantle of a learned link between the seekers of information and knowledge with their myriad sources. The most important aim is "Winning a Lifetime of Good Reading".

9.2. LIBRARY MISSION

Addressing a group of librarians, Dr.Abraham Kaplan (1918–93), the then President of the American Philosophical Association, asked the assembled to develop intimate commerce with the whole universe of knowledge, to achieve success in their profession; listen to his charming advice.

"Like your profession mine also has thrust upon it, as its appropriate domain, the whole world of knowledge, the whole of culture. Nothing is supposed to be foreign to us, and we ought to be prepared, under suitable circumstances, to be helpful with regard to any and every area of human concern."

Actually, we must all bear in mind that teaching, medicine and librarianship are neither jobs, nor even professions; they are essentially missions and librarians are missionaries. Yes, librarianship is a mission, no matter whether it is a School Library or an Academic Library or a Public Library or a Special library

Libraries offer opportunities for growth and self development. They help in exploring the minds' internal and external discoveries. based on intellectual inheritance. This is the ultimate mission for which libraries are striving.

9.3. PUBLIC LIBRARIES

Public libraries may be regarded as Centers of Learning. Highlighting this important role of libraries, the noted American poet, Karl Shapiro (1913-2000) while declaring open a Public Library, some years back, compared it to "...a school, college, or University, the teaching staff of which was on permanent vacation."

While the traditional educational institutions dole out information and knowledge based on a limited curriculum and prescribed textbooks, libraries introduce their users to the whole universe of knowledge, enabling them to 'travel terrain beyond textbooks' and graze in the wide pastures of literature and weave into the tapestry of their lives an ardent love for reading and an abiding interest in books.

An anonymous user who was benefited by making use of rich resources of a public library has paid a handsome tribute to it in the following words.

"My alma mater grants no degrees and holds no reunions for old grads. No matter, that is where I received my education. There in that old building, selecting my courses from a wide and unlimited curriculum, counseled, guided now and again by members of the Faculty, I spent hundreds of happy hours. There I received my education. A college or a University might have handed me a parchment attesting to an education of a sort, but for a truly liberal education, I give you, my alma mater - The Brownsville Branch of the Brooklyn Public Library."

— From an old grad.

Public library services are aimed at the entire community. It serves everyone uniformly irrespective of cast, creed, age and sex. However, children are highly favoured category of users for a public library. Developing and sustaining reading habit among children is a top priority function of public libraries.

The following are some of the practices of the 'Children's Sections' of public libraries in developed countries.

- Public libraries are providing extensions with pleasant parks, miniature zoos with live kittens, puppies, tantalizing toys etc.
- A grand and attractive variety of playthings are found in their children's sections.
- In order to improve children's literacy skills, additional activities like children's summer reading programmes and pre-school programmes are also being vigorously implemented.
- Parents are involved to instill love of books in children. Parents are told to adopt the role of promoters of reading among their children.
- Public libraries are requesting parents to send their children soon after they are able to talk and walk, to their libraries, where these tiny toddlers are introduced to colourfully produced children's books.
- Public libraries are also sending frequently to the Daycare Centers bags of children's new books, puppets and puzzles.
- Programmes like "Books for Little Hands, (sponsored by San Jose Public Library), "Raise A Reader" (started by the Vancouver Sun - a Company of Global Communication Corporation, Canada) are addressing children from age of two years.
- The children listen to nursery rhymes and stories. Storybooks are being read out, children's plays are staged, fancy dress programmes etc. are organized.

These ideas, if implemented, will go a along way in developing and sustaining reading habit among growing children.

9.4. INDIAN LIBRARY SCENARIO

In 2004, Nathan Allonby, an Engineer from the United Kingdom, visited India. He wrote a letter in *The Times of India* titled, 'Library Laxity', meaning less care or concern for libraries that play important roles in keeping the people of a democratic, developing country always enlightened. Given below is the text of his letter, which should serve as an eye-opener for the 'Powers - That Be'- in our country.

Library Laxity : "There is a shocking absence of Libraries in India, compared with the West, especially Europe. This will only restrict India's development.

It is surprising that the information strategy of the Government of India relies so completely on the Information Technology - IT, - an obsession represented by the bizarre example that India should give Cambodia Internet Terminals as development. As a professional Engineer in England, Information is the primary commodity of my business. In addition to my own technical resources, I belong to 3 libraries - 1 public, 1 private and a university library. This is absolutely essential to my work. Technical standards, professional journals, specialized textbooks, where else can these be obtained?

My own experience is that the Internet is primarily a medium of communication, rather than a knowledge resource. For the type of accurate, detailed and verifiable information required for professional application, there is no substitute yet for the printed word. While appreciating how much India has gained from IT, no one can deny that even software engineers write and use text books."(via email)

(*Times of India*: 6 December 2004.)

India needs to wipe out the severe dearth of public libraries all equipped with the most up-to-date internet connectivity etc., particularly in the rural areas. Whenever, this matter comes up for discussion someone or the other hijacks the attention to three other related issues, because these are very strongly associated with the status of public libraries in information age. These are outlined here.

Grim Power Situation is a major stumbling block in harnessing the benefits of the IT for the benefit of rural areas. Power supply enables IT which itself is an enabling technology. Thus, uninterrupted power supply is a prerequisite for any progress and cultural development in information age. Power supply is an important infrastructure. This problem has to be attended on war-footing.

Public libraries need IT support for providing high quality information services.

Poor Primary Education is the second major problem, of India and, for that matter, of all the developing countries. Primary education is not available to every child. In spite of imaginative programmes like *Saksharadeepa* – sponsored by Government of India and similar programmes by other State Governments, the number of literate people is not increasing commensurately. The rate of literacy as revealed by the 2001 census is 65.4%.

Primary education leads to literacy. Spread of literacy is like oxygen for public libraries. Public libraries survive on literacy or say, primary education.

Literacy rate is a perceptual number - people perceived to be literate. It is not an accurate indicator of the proportion of readers in the population, asserts Professor Brij Kothari, of the IIM, Ahmedabad, in his article entitled, 'Literate but Cannot Read'. A survey conducted by him in four Hindi States – Rajasthan, U.P., M.P. and Bihar revealed that out of the 68.7% literates only 26% could read a simple text of 35 words in Hindi, which a class III student would be expected to read. [Brij Kothari, "Literate but cannot read", *Times of India*, 22/2/08.] It is a sad situation.

Adult literacy in the sense of the *regular practice of reading* is perhaps better reflected in the dropout rate of 60%

of school goers. It leads later to the danger of these dropouts relapsing into functional illiteracy.

Prof.Brij Kothari, of IIM, Ahmedabad has initiated a innovative idea called Same Language Subtitling (SLS). SLS is currently being employed on television song programmes in India to encourage literacy skill improvement among the early literates. This ensures that reading becomes by-product of entertainment.

This peril could probably have been averted if the schools had good libraries, and if there were efficient public library units in the vicinity. Books teach us swiftly and successfully.

The establishment of the University Grants Commission (UGC) in 1956 and its National Assessment and Accreditation Council (NAAC) in 1994 have led to the resuscitation and revitalization of the universities and colleges in the country. Similar bodies are the need of the hour to take care of the school and the public library sectors.

According to Dr. Sanjiva Kaura, national coordinator of the National Alliance for the Fundamental Right to Education (NAFRE), a people's initiative, India needs immediately more than four lakhs (0.4 million) of schools and over 40 lakhs (4 million) of teachers.

Similarly going by the International Federation of Library Associations and Institutions (IFLA, The Hague, Netherlands) standards, India needs over four lakhs (0.4 million) of free public libraries equipped with the latest versions of the IT and personnel to manage them.

Prof. K.S.Deshpande proposes a few suggestions for improving public and school library situation, at macro level.

- The Raja Ram Mohan Roy Library Foundation, RRRLF (1972) needs to be urgently metamorphosed into the "Raja Rammohun Roy Public Library Grants Commission" (RRRPLGC or RPLGC), with powers and status akin to the UGC. A person of eminence should head the proposed RRRPLGC.

A similar body, "School Grants Commission" can be set up to vitalize and vivify the schools.

- A major structural change required is to shift 'Public Libraries' from the Concurrent List to the Central List. The Centre could be pressurized into enacting a single powerful public library Act, and transform India into a Land of Libraries.
- Our existing library related laws and even the Delivery of Books Act, are toothless and are incapable of delivering the goods. Suitable amendments have to be made.
- Then and then only, model public libraries would be established in each State of the Union, just like the central universities under the UGC.
- Russia and Cuba and probably China, which were in a condition identical to India at the dawn of their freedom banished illiteracy from their lands with lightening speed and librarized their territories with amazing alacrity. While Russia has a public library for every 700 people of its population, thousand and thousands of our people are without proper schools and public libraries.

After these micro and macro level initiations for academic and public libraries, we need to look at the shape and structure of reading habit in computer and telecommunication driven information society.

Part C :

Reading Habit in Internet Era

10
READING HABIT AND ICT

From stone inscriptions to writings on papyrus, vellum and parchment, palm leaves, birch bark and metals like copper plates, to the printed form, information has gone through several avatars, the latest being the electronic form through Information and Communication Technology (ICT). ICT encompasses, computers, digital communication, internet, all sorts of information -text, image, moving images, audio- available on the net and its electronic exploitation.

Every profession, every walk of life is influenced by ICT. Banking, insurance, travel, tourism, medicine, science and technology- well, every business is in one way or the other benefited by ICT. Every business is information business. Here the focus is on reading related issues.

ICT, to a very great extent, has solved the difficulties faced by librarians in storage and processing of information. It helps them in speedily providing pinpointed reference and information services. If all those in the library profession have not only to survive, but also prosper in this market-friendly, competitive, commercial era, they have to familiarize with ICT applications.

But how much of ICT application in a library is desirable? Perhaps the best person to answer this question is Professor F.W. Lancaster, an eminent British Librarian. In his address 'Have Libraries Really Gained from Technology?' at the Institute of Information Studies in Bangalore, (8 July 2002) Prof. Lancaster has highlighted the foibles or idiosyncrasies of the IT. Among other things, he quoted a user of an academic library who maintained that the web has 98% junk; he wanted the library and its officers to tell him where the 2% of valuable stuff was. Lancaster concluded his address thus:

"I believe that the chance of getting a reference question answered completely and correctly is lesser than it was 40 years ago. I liked the Library of 30 years ago much more than I like the automated Library of today. In the automated Library the human touch is missing. Dehumanization of Library service is not at all a desirable thing. It is like a baby being fed by a cold machine, instead of the warmth of the breast feeding."

It may be noted that it was the same Prof. Lancaster who propagated the idea of paperless society in mid-1950s. This 'U-turn' does not mean anything against ICT applications in library. It is a senior professional's appeal to exercise cautious enthusiasm in deciding how much of ICT is necessary and sufficient. He was trying to tell the difference between the dehumanized virtual library and culturally vibrant, community based library.

Similarly, Gordon Johnson in his article, "Web Vs the Library" asserts, "... Real libraries have the bonus of trained staff to help you find what you seek unlike most search engines which bombard you with unnecessary, extra, unwanted useless data."

Computer world is virtual and conventional librarianship is the real one. There is loneliness in digital world, but conventional librarianship is a community thing. There is a specific physical entity called library.

Library as a place has a great social value. On a university and college campuses library is a meeting place, place to exchange ideas. Similarly, public libraries are meeting points. But, the virtual libraries have speed, wide access etc.

Physical library is like idol worshiping. In computer based information, the God is a concept and not an idol with shape.

What we need is a blend of the two.

Historically, there are two sets views about the use of ICT with respect to reading and reading habit. There are conservative views, and there are overenthusiastic views.

10.1. TWO VIEWS AND THE TRUTH

Here is an attempt to give arguments, counter arguments and the truth regarding computer and reading related issues.

Argument: When in the 60's or 70's of the 20th century the computer burst upon the book world, there was loud talk that the book is dead. Everything will be available in the computer. There is no future for the book. People predicted *Paperless Society,* [It was a title by FW Lancaster.]

Counter Argument: Books can never be replaced by anything. Experience tells that for attaining greater attention span, for prolonged concentration, for enriching our vocabulary, for gaining fluency in language, for securing mastery over knowledge, for getting enlightenment, the book in its various avatars up to the present printed version, which has survived for nearly 600 years, is more reliable, dependable than the computer and the IT.

Truth:

- Worried about the future of the Book, the American Congress set up a Committee to go into the prospects of book. Given below is an extract from a paper by Morris Phillipson in the Report submitted by the Committee entitled *Books In Our Future: Perspectives and Proposals* edited by John Y Cole.1987.

  > "...We would be very foolish if we were to accept a sense of gloom from a belief that the conventional books and journals must be replaced by the images on a video terminal. We know for a fact that experiments conducted in that direction have not saved money...."

- Greater attention span for prolonged concentration is not possible while reading on computers, as it is straining our eyes. But, enriching vocabulary, gaining fluency in language, securing mastery over knowledge, getting enlightenment etc. are possible even in computer based reading. These are intrinsic in nature.
- Computer is a medium just as the book is a medium. Mere survival for nearly 600 years does not make book more reliable, dependable than the computer and the IT. There should not be any attachment with the medium. It is the content that makes it reliable or otherwise and not the medium.

Argument : In certain respects, the major advantage of the computer is its speed. One can get certain information faster than used to be possible earlier. But that is only information, not judgement. In some realms of human activity greater speed is not desirable, for example in being infused by a piece of music, or in savouring excellent food or in making love. What is the hurry about information available faster, if we have educated a class of people to make practical judgment that will keep us from being exploded to death.

Counter Argument: If speed is an asset of a computer, there is nothing wrong about that. To say that ICT gives only information and not judgement is incorrect. Even in case of book, it is not the paper or print medium which is giving the judgement, it is the author who gives. During elections or any current event is being discussed on the television, we are getting instantaneous expert opinions. You find both information and judgement with speed.

Truth: Consider about the National Budget. Till late 1980 we used to get scanty information about the national budget over radio or television, and full details were available only in the following day's newspaper. Now the full-text of the budget is made available on the internet as the finance minister starts reading it in the Parliament. The television media, user groups and blogs on internet start beaming their views/judgements. How reliable or valuable these views are, can be assessed by each individual.

Speed with which we get information is critical in case of natural or man-made calamities. This helps in disaster management etc.

Argument: It is dangerous to promote the illusion that you can get anything you want by sitting in front of a computer screen. It is arrogance and hubris. There is something charming about the book. You can carry it any where, read it anywhere, mark its pages and write down your reactions in the margins, in case it is your own book and not of a library

Counter Argument: That digital reading is not portable can no longer be accepted. Now it is possible to read an e-book or e-journal on your cell phone.

Truth: Most of the arguments against digital readings have been technologically solved. Reading digital material is as enjoyable as analogue reading. In fact there are more features in e-book readers. Supporters and admirers of IT thought that it would remove the limitations, inherent in conventional electronic document reading.

All these arguments, counter arguments and truths are presented here just to see that a gullible reader is not caught in these academic discussions. He/She should know that such discussions are inevitable whenever any change is introduced in society. Now we must accept that computers, ICT are here to stay, and we have to harness its strength. The arguments such as books are better than web based information is no longer valid. Each reader has to use his judgement and be responsible for using a particular type resource.

Instead of thinking about the ICT versus Book, we must see how publishing world is benefited by ICT. It used to take at least two-three years to bring out a book. Now it is possible to publish a book in less than two months time. Authors, editors, illustrators, publishers, printers, distributors, booksellers have been benefited by ICT. The cost of book production is reduced. Time required for publication is drastically reduced.

No wonder, the number of books published is increasing with every passing year and publishing has grown into a major industry. Instead of the book fading away, it has been flourishing on a greater and grander scale. Millions of books are coming out of the presses of the world.

10.2. READING MATERIAL ON THE WEB

There is too much to read on the web. But not everything on the web is worth reading. These are not reliable sources. Any Tom, Dick, Harry, Mary, Jane, Susan can write anything and put it on the web. Therefore, it is better to evaluate each website, before using. You can get the method of evaluation of website also on the web. Generally, authority, scope, content, utility, special features and navigability are the criteria.

If you want reliable sources find a subject gateway and search in it. Subject gateways are collections of websites which are evaluated, selected and organized by subject experts and/ or librarians and/ or information specialists.

In addition, there is substantial information on practically any subject. Although people access internet, but not many people know how to search pinpointed information. Although training programmes can be organized for this, it is better one learns on his own by reading the help option of different search engines and directories.

There are websites exclusively meant for certain groups of users, such as kids. Animated stories from **Panchtantra, Aesop's Fables, Akbar-Birbal, Vikram-Betal, sites to teach mathematics, English grammar, how different things work (eg.: car, rocket, airplane), why certain things happen (eg: rainbow, eclipse, earthquake, tsunami etc), etiquettes and manners, ... you name it and you have it.**

You can get information about books, movies etc. You can access free e-journals and, e-books etc. In addition, you must visit the following libraries available online.

- The Internet Public Library (www.ipl.org/)
- The WWW Virtual Library (http:/ / vlib.org/)
- The Online Book Page (http:/ / onlinebooks.library.upenn. edu/)
- Public Library of Science (http:/ / www.plos.org/)
- The World Digital Library (http:/ / www.wdl.org/ en/)

Each one of these e-libraries is a digital gateway to many other sources, such as encyclopaedias, dictionaries, abbreviation dictionaries etc. Similarly, there are sites for home remedies, Medical information resources like PubMed is freely found on the net.

Internet is a large store of many images, portraits, paintings, maps, songs, clippings, tutorials, PowerPoint presentations etc. All these are different types of information resources.

There are many full-text e-journals and e-books available on the net. Most of the classics whose copyright is expired are available on line freely or for some nominal payment. Famous masterpieces are available in many languages.

It is often told that reading continuously on the computer is strenuous to eyes. The other complaints are regarding electricity dependency, difficulty in scrolling up and down etc.

Many of the difficulties of reading e-books are solved by introduction of a device called E-Book Reader. The following features are found in an e-book reader.

- You can get the feel of turning pages forward and backward instead of scrolling up or down.
- You can adjust illumination and gray-scale.
- You can adjust magnification to suit your sight.
- The reader is portable; it is almost of the size of a notebook.
- It runs on battery when you are out.
- You can bookmark any page.
- You can refer a built-in dictionary for any unfamiliar word and get back to the text.
- You can make notes while reading by opening some other window.
- You can write reference to any specific part of the text to be quoted.

- You may copy any portion or your notes on to any word processing file.

For a genuine reader, both ICT and paper based readings are equally important. Both have their values. Both can coexist, just as movies and TV industries are growing with each others support.

In the knowledge society of today, information has assumed the role of the most basic, most important and most valuable commodity. Information forms the very bedrock of our day-to-day life. Every member of the society, from the tiny toddler, to the man in dotage, has necessarily to have information. While the IT happens to be the magic lamp for quick retrieval of information, the chief sources of information and knowledge are reliable books and journals, and they promote lifelong learning from the moment of conception to the time of cremation or birth to burial.

Finally, it is necessary to state a few truths which are significant to the mission of developing and sustaining reading habit in the information age.

- We should not be lost in the glamour and grandeur of technology. ICT is only an enabling technology. The reader should focus on information, i.e. on 'Putting the I in IT'. That is the need of the hour. [Curtsey: Thomas Davenport. 2000. "Putting the I in IT" in *Mastering Information Management* Edited by Donald Marchand *et al. Financial Times* and Prentice Hall.]
- Our children must not only be literates, but also have mastery over computer and information literacy.
- There is more to read now than ever before. There was a time when getting information was a problem. But now information overload is the problem.
- Information overload includes phone calls, E-mails, Print Media, multi-media, social-networking etc.

- Along with speed reading we must acquire skills of handling information overload. (Please type "handling information overload" in the search box of any search engine like Google and get useful information from the internet.

Handling information overload reduces stressful moments and helps in getting competitive professional edge. Development and sustenance of reading habit is the core success factor, no matter what is your profession, no matter what is your age.

Stressing the importance of lifelong learning, Prof Deshpande had narrated an instance. A University graduate after receiving his parchment at the convocation called on the vice-chancellor to bid him farewell and also to seek his blessings. "Sir', he said "By the grace of God and your own benediction, I have completed my education." The Vice-chancellor's reply was not only crisp but cathartic also. He said, "Young man, congratulations on completing your studies; but look at me, I have just begun my education."

XXX

If we want to be counted in life, we have to go on continuously and carefully polishing our minds by reading and writing, and thereby leave our footprints on the sands of time. In these inspiring words, I see the reflections of the seventh habit ['Sharpen the saw'] of Stephen Covey's *Seven Habits of Highly Effective People* with which we began this book.

Select Quotations About Reading

Reading is the best medicine for a sick man, the best music for a sad man, the best counsel for a desperate man, the best comfort for one afflicted. — **John Florio**

It is often said that one has but one life to live, but that is nonsense. For one who reads, there is no limit to the number of lives that may be lived, for fiction, biography, and history offer an inexhaustible number of lives in all periods of time. — **Louis L'Amour**

A book is a gift you can open again and again.

— **Garrison Keillor**

Books are the quietest and most constant of friends; they are the most accessible and wisest of counselors, and the most patient of teachers. — **Charles William Eliot**

Miss a meal if you have to, but don't miss a book.

— **Jim Rohn**

People die, but books never die. No man and no force can abolish memory. — **Franklin D. Roosevelt**

When you read with your children, you show them that reading is important, but you also show them they're important — that they are so important to you that you will spend 20 minutes a day with your arm around them.

— Laura Bush

Research shows us that children who read from a very early age are more likely to begin reading themselves at an early age. They're more likely to excel in school. They're more likely to graduate secondary school and go to college.

— Laura Bush

Books are the carriers of civilization. Without books, history is silent, literature dumb, science crippled, thought and speculation at a standstill. They are engines of change, windows on the world, lighthouses erected in the sea of time.

— Barbara W. Tuchman

Without books God is silent, Justice dormant, Science at a standstill, Philosophy lame, Literature dumb; and everything else is plunged in Cimmerian darkness.

— Thomas Bartholin

Reading without reflection is like eating without digesting. **— Edmund Burke**

Books are men of higher stature

And the only men that speak louder

For further times to hear. **— Robert Browning**

A good book is the precious life-blood of a master-spirit, embalmed and treasured upon purpose, to a life beyond life. **— John Milton**

Read, Read, and then Read some more. Always Read. Find the voices that speak most to YOU. This is your pleasure and blessing, as well as responsibility! **— Naomi Shihab Nye**

A good book is the best of friends, the same today and forever. **— Martin Tupper**

You think your pains and heartbreaks are unprecedented in the history of the world, but then you read. It was books that taught me that the things that tormented me were the very things that connected me with all the people who were alive, or who have ever been alive.

— James Baldwin

I suggest that the only books that influence us are those for which we are ready, and which have gone a little further down our particular path than we have yet got ourselves.

— E. M. Forster

A bookstore is one of the only pieces of evidence we have that people are still thinking. **— Jerry Seinfeld**

A good book should leave you ... slightly exhausted at the end. You live several lives while reading it.

— William Styron

A real book is not one that we read, but one that reads us. **— W. H. Auden**

A truly great book should be read in youth, once again in maturity and once more in old age, as a fine building should be seen by morning light, at noon and by moonlight.

— Robertson Davies

The reading of all good books is like a conversation with the finest minds of past centuries. **— Rene Descartes**

Reading maketh a full man,
Conference a ready man, and
Writing an exact man.
Some books are to be tasted,
Be swallowed, and
Some few to be chewed and digested.

— Francis Bacon

To read is to empower: to empower is to write; to write is to influence; to influence is to change; to change is to live.

— Jane Evershade

If there is a book you really want to read but hasn't been written yet, then you must write it. **— Tony Morrison**

The habit of reading is one of the greatest resources of mankind. **— William Lyon Phelps**

Books are of the people, by the people, for the people. Literature is the immortal part of history; and it is the best and the most enduring part of personality.

— William Lyon Phelps

When you give someone a book, you don't give him just paper, ink, and glue. You give him the possibility of a whole new life. **— Christopher Morley**

The greatest gift is a passion for reading. It is cheap, it consoles, it distracts, it excites, it gives you knowledge of the world and experience of a wide kind. It is a moral illumination. **— Elizabeth Hardwick**

What is reading but a silent conversation?

— Walter Savage Landor

Today a reader, tomorrow a leader. **—W. Fusselman**

I believe in the absolute and unlimited liberty of reading. I believe in wandering through the stacks and picking out the first thing that strikes me. I believe in choosing books based on the dust jacket. **— Rick Moody**

I cannot see that lectures can do so much good as the reading of the books from which the lectures are taken.

— Dr. Samuel Johnson

Those who do not read can have nothing to think and little to say. **— Dr. Samuel Johnson**

To read is to fly; it is to soar to a point of vantage which gives a view over wide terrains of history, human variety, ideas, shared experience and the fruits of many inquiries.

— Alberto Manguel

Children Read Because They Want To, Not Because They Have To. **— Laura J. Colker**

The things I want to know are in books. My best friend is the man who will give me a book. **— Abraham Lincoln**

No man can be truly educated in life, unless he is a reader of books. **— Benjamin Franklin**

A room without books is like a body without soul."

— Cicero (106-43 B.C.)

Select Bibliography

(It excludes the sources cited in the text)

Adler, Mortimer Jerome Adler and Van Doren, Charles; *How to Read a Book*. Revised Ed. New York, Simon & Schuster, 1997.

Bloom, Harold; *How to Read and Why*. New York, Simon & Schuster, 2000

Broom, M. E. and Others; *Effective Reading Instruction*. New York, McGraw Hill 1951.

Buzan, Tony; *Speed Reading*. 3rd ed. Plume Book, 1991.

Dechant, Emerald V. and Smith, Henry; *Psychology in Teaching Reading*. 2nd Ed. Englewood Cliff, Prentice Hall, 1977.

Manguel, Alberto; *A History of Reading*. London, Flamingo, an Imprint of Harper Collins, 1996.

Menzel, Emil W.; *Suggestions for the Teaching of Reading in India*. London, Humphrey Milford, 1944.

Menzel, Emil and others. Ed.; *Teaching of Reading*. London, OUP, 1966

Murray, W and Downes, L. W.; *Children Learn to Read: The Play-Learn Approach*. London, George G Harrap LG, 1955

O'Brien, Geoffrey; *Browser's Ecstasy: A Meditation on Reading.* Washington, Counterpoint, 2000.

Osen, Diane Ed.; *The Book that Changed My Life.* New York, The Modern Library, 2002.

Otto, Wayne and Chester, Robert D.; *Objective Based Reading.* Reading, Addison-Wesley, 1976.

Pitkin, Walter B.; *Art of Rapid Reading: A Book For People Who Want to Read Faster and More Accurately.* New York, McGraw Hill, 1929 [Hardback Kessinger 2008]

Schonell, Fred J.; *Psychology ana Teaching of Reading.* 4th Ed. Edinburgh, Oliver and Boyd. 1961.

Smith, Donald E. P.; *Learning to Read and Write: A Task Analysis.* New York, Academic Press, 1976.

Smith, Donald E. P.; *Technology of Reading and Writing.* New York, Academic Press, 1976.

Staiger, Ralph C. Ed.; *The Teaching of Reading.* Paris, Unesco, 1973.

Taylor, Insup and Taylor, M Martin; *Psychology of Reading.* New York, Academic Press, 1983.

Willes Margaret; *Reading Matters.* London, Yale University Press, 2008.

NAME INDEX

E

F

G

H

I

J

K

L

M

N

O

P

R

S

T

Title Index

Titles Mentioned in this Book

[Books, Journals, Magazines and Movies]

INDEX